IT'S YOUR CHOICE

Words Spoken to a Young Chiropractor

IT'S YOUR CHOICE

Words Spoken to a Young Chiropractor

Dr. William M. Harris
Chiropractic Philanthropist
With
Thomas Outler Morgan, DC
Collaborator

fW Publishing / Marietta GA

It's Your Choice ..
Words Spoken to a Young Chiropractor ©2011
Dr. William M. Harris
Dr. Thomas Outler Morgan, DC

For Information, please address:
FW Publishing Company
P.O. Box 93 / Marietta, GA 30061-0093
Email: fwpublishing@earthlink.net
website: www.griffinpublishinggroup.com

Library of Congress Control Number: 2011932758

ISBN: 978-0-9827994-4-4

Printed in the United States of America

Thomas Outler Morgan, DC
Collaborator's Note:

William M. Harris, DC, passed away November 9, 2008 at ninety years young. Although he hoped to live well beyond his 100th birthday just like his sister, an unfortunate fall and resulting complications interfered.

He is deeply missed by all who knew him, and especially by those fortunate to have known him well, but Dr. Harris ensured his presence would be felt in the chiropractic profession forever. He is the most generous benefactor chiropractic has ever known.

William Harris was born in the Deep South into rural, upper class society, but suffered profound loss as a young boy. His mother became mentally ill and had to be institutionalized. His father became incapacitated after losing his crops and fortune to the boll weevil.

Young Bill went to live with his sister and grew up with the Boutwell family. His early life was a search for identity and a struggle to come to terms with the absence of parental love. Those early experiences created a soft place in his heart for orphans and he grew to love helping young people, particularly young chiropractors.

No one was more successful in chiropractic than Dr. Harris. His fame spread from Georgia all over the south and soon doctors from near and far were coming to his weekly "sessions." These early coaching sessions led him to become a premier consultant in the profession, launching *Practice Consultants* and building it over three decades into a highly successful business.

The success of his business enabled him to create the non-profit Foundation for the Advancement of Chiropractic Education (FACE) to fund his philanthropic endeavors. He was financially frugal and wanted all his clients to be big savers and to give back through the "hole you receive from."

A man of his word, Bill began donating more generously to chiropractic education than anyone ever had before him. I was honored to help him structure his gifts to both Palmer College of Chiropractic and Life University. Today, as a member of the FACE Board, it has been my privilege to work with Bill's friends to bring to fruition his dreams of supporting the grants and gifts he had started. "Going on in perpetuity" — those were some of the last words I ever heard him say.

Many times throughout our decades-long friendship, I urged Bill to write a book about his life. He insisted the book instead focus on his coaching methods so it would help young chiropractors maintain their passion and dedication to the profession, just as he did for so many, many years. I cherish the many hours spent with Bill, asking him questions and listening as he sternly projected his ideas on tape. He promised to push the record button in the middle of the night whenever he felt the innate call to dictate some important information for this project.

One of the last projects Bill committed his energy and money to was at Life University in Marietta, Georgia where he served on the Board of Trustees until his death. Bill selected Life University to remember him after his death and asked his good friend and University president, Guy Riekeman, DC, to make a place for him on campus. Today, his memorabilia, marker and remains are enshrined on campus and in Life's chiropractic history museum.

Following his death, the members he appointed to his board of directors founded the "Red Hat Scholarship" in Bill's honor and in recognition of his ever-present red cap. The interest from these contributions will be given each year to a qualified Life University student and awarded at an annual "Red Hat Day" on campus to commemorate Dr. Harris's life and all he did for the University.

I am honored to have played a small part in making this book a reality and give special thanks to my wife, Mary Ann, for her editing and suggestions. I always said it was Mary Ann's award- winning cooking Bill enjoyed far more than my friendship. Thank you Bill for your friendship and all you have done for Mary Ann and me, as well as the profession.

"Read a little along each day," is what Bill advised doctors and chiropractic students to do with this work, "so something chiropractic will be with you every day." Enjoy.

Thomas Outler Morgan, DC
Mary Ann (Kalb) Morgan
Cedartown, Georgia

My favorite poem
Quoted by Dr. Harris at every speech he delivered. . .

Wages

"I bargained with life for a penny
And life would pay me no more,
However I cried at eventide
As I counted my scanty store.
For life is a just employer
He gives you what you ask;
But once you have set the wages,
Why you must bear the task.
I worked for menial's hire,
Only to learn, dismayed,
That any wage I had asked,
Life would have gladly paid."

—Author unknown—

TABLE of CONTENTS

I

Do Your Best . . . Forget the Rest

I'm rolling out of bed this morning, early as usual. I can think most clearly early on now. Like most mornings, I rise alone. Sitting on the side of the bed I stare at the day from these old eyes of mine. There is no physical inventory to take stock of; nothing will please me much there anyway. It's the inner man I know, not this wrinkled figure.

Disciplines: that must be my first action. Yes Bill, think disciplines; get up and get at it. Don't think about your mood, or that doctor who said you were a manic depressive. I don't buy it. I do get down, way down, but I always come back up. Don't confuse yourself, Bill. Concentrate on first things first. Pray!

God, give me another day to help some of your people. Make it another great day; let me do something special. I pray not to have an average life. Continue to help me make a difference in people's lives. Help me use my wealth to change the world through chiropractic. I know all I have is a blessing from You Lord. You have always blessed me and given me more than most people could ever spend or use. Still, money is no comfort unless I remind myself that You have a plan and purpose for me, a place where You can use me today. I know that is one of the reasons why I am still here. Yes, I'll blurt it out — there is a place for me today in God's order! Amen.

I find myself talking to God more these days. It seems life comes down to where He is my only real helper. I just had a thought; I will teach someone today that prayer works powerfully when you pray for what you know is the will of God. I would never pray to win the lottery. Instead, I pray to accomplish something bigger than myself.

Lord, I want to know even more where strength and power originates.

I know my weaknesses all too well . . . my lack of talent, my laziness, my prejudices. You can make something happen today, Bill. I have to keep pushing that record button and get on with this book. I can see it in every young chiropractor's hands.

I'm fighting back the negative thoughts now. BOOM! I have to detonate each one like those anti-aircraft shells over Baghdad! I can't move ahead in service if I think about my aches and negativity, my self-centeredness, or my loneliness. Get busy doing your exercise, Bill. I'm standing up now and doing those deep knee bends, standing on one leg. I can't do that one so well now.

I'm thinking about getting to the office and about today's schedule. "Do It" days and daily "Do It" lists still must be my big theme. I've got to take my own advice. It's time to motivate myself. I used this action strategy for the hundreds of doctors I helped in my consulting business. It works for old farts too.

Why does that seem so long ago? Boy, I was persistent, staying on their cases. I made sure they planned their work and worked their plan. I have to do the same today. I have to motivate myself above and beyond myself. I have to have a purpose and a focus. I have to be looking for "more fish to fry." But, there is always that negative, dark cloud moving across my mind. BOOM! That thought is blasted away.

God, help me lick these demons today.

I have myself to contend with, the self that wants to give credit to my aches and pains this morning. I'll turn my mind to putting those millions to work in the right place, doing the right things. I'm fighting that self that gets angry for no reason, the self that wants to make excuses why I should not just roll over in this bed and feel sorry for my sorry self. No! I'll get going now! Positive self talk is a big key to keeping an aging man going.

I'm driving this old car to the office again. There's no sense wasting money on a new car.

Keep me safe, Lord.

The law of averages is not so good for us older drivers in Atlanta. It won't do to look at the dents and scrapes already on this old trap. Great things come into my mind when I'm driving. I also get these flash thoughts at night when I am half sleeping. BJ taught me to keep that pad and pen next to the bed (BJ Palmer called his inspirations "flash thots") and wake up and write down these great "thots."

Are they from innate? I don't know, but I am getting a great one now! There has to be a lesson in this somewhere. Maybe it is because my mind is busy with driving so the spirit can come through to me. I need some help with my mind. My staff, Jane, watches me closely now as I try to dial the phone. I keep getting wrong numbers and mixed up. I don't know if this is aging but it is sure frustrating and stirs up my anger voice!

The other day I was haranguing a person on the phone who I thought owed me money. On and on I went until he got a word in edgeways. It was not even the guy I thought I was calling. I see my family and staff laughing at these foolish things I do now. I deserve these laughs; before my dotage, they wouldn't have dreamed of laughing at me.

I was such a control person before that I could not stand stupid things . . . now I are one! I guess I have to learn to laugh at myself. Maybe I am loosening up? Why was I always so stiff and insistent that others perform perfectly? I'm still working on my coaching huh? I guess I have their laughs coming, as I was too hard on them and me!

I can't dwell on my goof ups at this stage. It's not easy trying to learn how I can laugh at myself. What was my favorite charge for new doctors? . . . do your (my) best and forget the rest!

II

You Are as Good as Any, And Better than Most!

If I ever had a theme song as a consultant, this was it. I had every doctor repeat it in the mirror every day he or she was under my coaching: *You are as good as any, and better than most!* Many were living in defeat'ville. Some had such low self esteem I knew they needed the most help. I was on a mission to find out how they had gotten so low.

I knew from my early life that growing up without a mother meant no encouragement and low self esteem. I was not a popular kid, but I always wanted to fit in somehow. I wanted many friends, but all through my life I kept so private. I just couldn't give myself away in friendship. Maybe it was because, like my parents, I thought that one day friends would leave me.

What I think God did give me as a young man was an ability to "read" people's motives, their intent and how much they would work and sacrifice to achieve success. I knew that everything I wanted just didn't fall into place. There was no substitute for hard work. I found out a secret to success for me — I had to pick one thing I could do and then do it with all my heart. When it turned out well, something happened deep inside my soul. There was a value point to grow on.

Even though I was successful, I still had to force the

negative, low self esteem out of my mind. I didn't know much about deserving to be successful in life. I was never taught that concept. All you have to do is watch the news (it's all bad of course). You will see too many people struggling with their great negatives.

When I read Napoleon Hill's *Think and Grow Rich* I knew where my thought life needed to be. Add that to what I learned from the Holy Bible as a deacon in a Baptist church in Albany, Georgia and you have Bill Harris's secrets to success. Many people have great talents, believing they deserve everything good. Still, they wind up with the other drug addicts on those cold steel trays in the city morgue. I spent a lifetime defeating my demons, but you must break this cycle of defeatism to move forward in life. That is why I had all my classes stand up and repeat, **"I'm as good as any, and better than most!"**

After achieving small victories myself, I started a system to be thankful for my little achievements. I didn't know the bar would be moved up and up to greater achievements.

I wanted to know the feeling of a valuable life. It is in the moment. So, make each moment count. It is there waiting for you to be involved. Don't be wishing or daydreaming of what it could be; get busy and make it happen. Ask God to still your mind and focus on the moment. You can't start too fast, and you may have to fly blind. You will not always see the end from the beginning, but you must feel it coming.

Sometimes, like me, you have to take a step of faith to get started. Small steps of greatness can turn into leaps and bounds! Remember, when you fall back in your old negative patterns and "stinkin thinking" you must regroup and try again. Here is the next positive point for you to say in the mirror each morning.

"The me that I see, is the me that I'll BE."

The doctors I helped in our Practice Consultants program who had the smallest practices usually felt they were not worthy at some point. The key to bringing them forward to success was in getting them to feel good about themselves, chiropractic, their towns and their futures. Healthy self es-teem means that, on a deeper level, they had to believe they were good doctors and good people (not perfect, but good) and that they were loved by God and other people. Then, they could believe they had positive value as people.

If they really believed they were, "As good as any, and better than most," they could move out of their ruts. I wanted them to think on this great truth all of their lives.

This next doctrine of success may be even bigger. Take this test:

If I asked you if someone is ten times more successful than you, does it mean that person is ten times smarter than you? No! Does it mean he or she works ten times harder than you? No! So, if someone is ten times more successful than you, then that person tends to **think** ten times **higher** than you. You see, it's not the size of your brain that makes you successful — **it's the size of your thinking and actions that count most**.

If I could leave you, young chiropractors, with one thing that would stay with you all your life, it would be the gift of **thinking big**! All great people have felt small and worthless, but they never let their big dreams go. Keep your dreams alive. I still write mine down and go over them when I feel the velvet touch of depression. Remember, when you have no answers for the smallness you feel inside, push on. Some-how, make yourself think big. I don't mean the huge ego, bragging type of big. I mean the quiet, hard working achiev-ing type. Read about successful people everyday; all of them experienced hard times, perhaps it just means that you also are on track for great success?

The great poet and author Ralph Waldo Emerson was born in abject poverty, was blind for several years and al-most died of lung disease. But, he said, "Great men are those who see that thoughts rule the world."

Other great thinkers have said:

"The mind is its own place, and in itself, can make a heaven
of hell, or a hell of heaven." —John Milton—

"There's neither good nor bad, except thinking makes it so."
—William Shakespeare—

"Nurture your mind with great thoughts, for you will never
go any higher than you think." —Benjamin Disraeli—

"The thought is the ancestor of the deed. If you precondition
your mind with thoughts of success, the deeds of success
naturally tend to follow." —Norman Vincent Peale—

What I want you to do while you are reading this chapter
is to stop, get a pen and write down the biggest ideas and
thoughts you can have about God, your family, your practice, the chiropractic profession and your life. You have to
think big to live big. Now, Do It!!

Here is one of my favorites:

"Make no little plans;
They have no magic to stir the soul.
Make big plans and with this be BOLD."
(Unknown author)

Great happiness comes from accomplishing big things. A
big income is a reward for your big efforts, nothing more
(remember it is never how much you make but only how
much you **save**). Mastering big practices brings more life
and health to more people. You get big respect and keep big
friends. As BJ said many times, "The real joy is in the climb,
not when you reach the mountaintop." Learn today how to
give away great love. The big love you give away is the big
love you keep.

*"Those who doubt, go without.
Those who believe, achieve!"*

I'm talking about filling up your working days with all
the patients you can adjust. Boredom must not find itself in
your office. Doctors today play on the Internet instead of us-

ing office time to seek more patients to serve. I used to catch my associates reading theme magazines and books about their hobbies. These are your greatest practice years. This is your stage and your time to shine. Oh sure, there is a certain amount of boredom doing the same thing every day. But, I know from experience, you have to focus on making your daily journey more cerebral and spiritual to avoid boredom.

If you have the right intent in your heart and mind, your days are great symphonies of love and service. You get caught up in caring for patients who want to feed from your chiropractic experience. That experience is what I have been talking about here. Make your practice and life a **big** experience. It must reflect all your love and dedication to chiropractic and to getting people subluxation-free.

Chiropractic was made great by those chiropractors who came before you who believed they would somehow change the world one patient at a time. They kept this faith even though they would not see much political fruit in their lifetimes. The same positive feedback for these old times (appreciative patients) must keep you fired up for the future of chiropractic. You are the one today who must make it happen for the next generation. Our future is based on you now. Take down those testimonials and those cured cases; they have always been the reason we are progressing. We are still evolving to the point that natural health care is becoming more important than pills.

Take it one patient at a time, doctor, and never quit. You can do this and you have to do it in a BIG WAY! So . . . Do It!

Let the Eagle Land

I picked out the American eagle as the symbol for our corporation, Practice Consultants Inc. I gave the Eagle Award to doctors who went way above the success point they ever expected to reach. Like our great nation, the eagle is the symbol of expansive beauty, awesome power and success to me. The eagle is the master of the sky. The next time you are in the valley of your hopes and dreams, look up at the eagle. You will see its majestic form lifting on some warm thermal drafts, spreading its great wings and gliding along in harmony with the world. Be that eagle, doctor. Soar and climb with me today.

> "My friend, if your hopes and dreams are starting to die,
> Be like the eagle, when it learns to fly.
> If your dreams have come true, but you're starting to tire,
> Be like the condor, and then fly even higher."

Now, here is my last poem I wrote to inspire myself and my friends:

Six Short Words

> So many people quit each day,
> And try again no more.
> They say there's no way to success
> They've tried it all before.
> But I'll keep on, and on, and on,
> And if you ask me why?
> I'll answer you in six short words.
> I HAVE JUST BEGUN TO FLY.

The Story of the Treasure Map

Every doctor and spouse enrolled in a new class with Practice Consultants was required to make a treasure map. I asked them to cut out pictures of everything they wanted in life and mount them on a large board. Everything they might ever want — clinics, equipment, vacations, house plans, offices — everything they might ever want in life on a material plane was included.

The reason this little exercise works is because we are mostly visual people. By creating a treasure map and looking at it a few minutes each day, you stimulate your creative mind and imagination to go to work generating ideas and solutions and fulfilling your dreams. In our first session with new doctors, we had to teach them how to create their treasure maps. I had them put these maps in their office dark room or some private place where they could see them every day. The stories I have to tell you from this action still astound me! Now, read these two paragraphs again three times and then go out and buy a large foam board. Do it!

The Future of Chiropractic

I don't have a crystal ball, but I know this to be true. Chiropractic is only as great as the chiropractors of the era. I look around me today and meet with all the college presidents and the technique and seminar teachers with this thought in mind. It is their era now. Where will they take us? Will it be where we need to go?

I have positive prayers for the profession. I am affirming right now the greatness of chiropractic and how we will proceed to capture the entire natural healing market. I embrace change. Change is at my core. If you are reading this and I am no longer walking this earth, know that I am with you young chiropractor. Also, know that you can make a difference. You are more important as a healer than you think. Recruit your children to be chiropractors and keep the legacy going forward. We need new blood, new ideas and new chiropractors. Always keep new ideas to think about and act upon. They keep me fresh and excited. The past is over, so I will learn new things and motivate myself with hope for today and tomorrow.

Recently I was honored at the Parker Seminar. I can't keep these "major awards" straight. There were thousands of chiropractors there. I met many new leaders and many doctors I had known and coached for many years. I'm keeping my antennae up all the time looking at the hearts of our chiropractic leaders and politicians. I never wanted to be in their shoes. Politics scared me: too much squeeze put on a fellow. Many of our politicians are great at their jobs, but I wonder whether they burn with the commitment to our chiropractic principles? I wonder if they really want to push us ahead as a separate and distinct science, art and philosophy?

Every group wants to mix with the medical profession because this brings more money and prestige, but does it allow freedom and the drugless voice to be heard? It needs to be heard and we are the ones who lead the way to natural health.

Yes, I have great appreciation for our chiropractic politicians, but I look at their hearts and their intent and I always read between the lines because I want to know if they really see us in a special place or if they just want us to join ranks with the medics? Do they burn with the feeling that from the adjustment you get life and that turning on the innate power inside patients is connected to our greatness? No other group will say the "real" doctor is inside the patient the way we say it. No one else says this but us, so I want to know about their commitment to this principle. I want to know their dreams and feel their intent. It has to be worth far more than their salaries. These thoughts are about our future. It has to be for the betterment of humankind.

Chiropractic is not for the chiropractors. It is for humankind. It is much bigger than us. I think that is why we have chiropractic. I think that is why you and I are chiropractors. I advise every young chiropractor who has the burning desire to see this profession reach its rightful place to build a large practice. After you see the miracles as a clinician and burn with the intensity to spread chiropractic to the world, then you can get involved in the profession's politics. Then you can get a job in your local and national associations, run for office and carry the heartbeat of a soldier, willing to give your all. I keep a sideways eye on our politicians who never had successful practices. Are their goals personal? This is important, because I believe this must be for chiropractic. So get involved doctor, work on unity, equality with other providers and getting more grants for our research.

I believe all chiropractors belong in a congress together, even though we are two parties, conservative and liberal. It has worked in the U.S. Congress, so it can work for us. Some ask me about unity and I ask them if the churches have unity? Are they together? A lot are splitting up as we speak. Still, I think God is using religions to draw people to Him and to seeing other people as more important than themselves. Religion's basic message is the same: that there is a God and He created us and we must have a response of faith.

So, I have hope that chiropractic will move forward with unity. In chiropractic, we can all agree on the central things — subluxation adjusting and healing principles. Even in confusion, though, I believe we chiropractors can get together. Medicare put our subluxation language in Federal law. I am still amazed that, when this happened, every college and research department didn't start the programs rolling to keep validating the subluxation. Someone tell me why the opposite is true?

Let's get back to my faith in our future. I see the leaders in our profession who were a nemesis to unity in the past era. They are now fading out of the picture. This gives me great hope that this new era will be one of our greatest in history. I am an eternal optimist. I want you to be one too. I was like that in practice, I always felt innate was changing my patients for the better after the adjustment. I want to always believe that God controls history and that He knows our future. Our job is to be obedient to what we know is true, what is right, and make sure this is how we serve our patients.

I see new attitudes and new leaders coming on the scene who have power and resolve. I also see greedy political groups trying to snare the profession monetarily by controlling colleges and continuing education and even what is taught. Also, I don't see why the national board keeps adding on more parts and costing our student doctors more and more. As my friend BJ used to say, "When is enough, enuf?" I still do not think these small, controlling groups will win in the end. Let me write this note to remind myself that on the Harris Trust Board the members will not succeed themselves after their term is over. They must stay off for one year. I want new ideas and leadership to prevail.

I believe progress will come along with our research and our viability and how we care for patients will be better understood and will qualify us for our rightful place in this world. Greatness is at hand! I want to count everyone who is proud of this profession. We can all make a difference. Stand up and be counted!

III

Determined Persistence is the Key to Lasting Achievement
(my favorite line!)

I want to tell you to **never** quit, even if you don't think you are destined to succeed. But, before I can give you that advice and tell you about the many people I've helped and my gift for spotting those in need, I first have to tell you something of myself. These are to be some of my last words, so I want to be very candid with myself, and with you.

I'll take it from the beginning. July 28, 1918 may seem like antiquity to the young chiropractic students reading this. But that year I was wrapped in silk baby clothes and later took my first steps in "high cotton." That meant my folks were well off and Dad was in his prime, smiling wide every day as he managed his workers and looked at those cotton bales, what southerners called "white gold," resting on our loading dock.

He never did any manual labor that I ever saw. He was born into a wealthy farmer's family. We had over two thousand acres of prime land seven miles outside of Opelika, Alabama. My brother still runs some of that farm today as this land has been in our family for over two hundred years. Dad never wore overalls. He was into management only. Instead, he wore a tie every day and managed his share croppers and hired hands.

I don't remember that first "great" war, but they needed cotton and we were shipping it and living in that big house on the edge of our plantation. My grandfather had purchased the land from the Creek Indians. When I can remember scenes from those days, I see myself reaching up for the loving arms of a mother who could not take me up in her lap or hold me.

I remember how funny her eyes looked before they took her away and committed her to the state hospital. She stared out past me to an unknown place. That did not stop my soul from hungering for her love, but it would never come. Even as an infant, I knew in the depths of my being that things were going to be very hard before they got soft.

No one talked of mental illness at that time and place. Doctors and family could commit the insane to an institution and, like my Mom, many never returned from their mental bondage. Dad would sometimes drive his big Packard up to Montgomery and bring Mom back for the day, but mostly she would sit and just smile when I tried to talk to her. I was Mary's last child. It was late in life for them so my older sister had to take over the job of raising me when my mom was taken away.

When my sister married H.B. Boutwell, I became like their stepchild. I played with their children when they came along. They were like little brothers to me. I made chiropractors out of these boys eventually. To date, we have 13 members of our family who are chiropractors. Losing both my parents, though, made me afraid to really have a solid relationship. My friends are many but my intimate friends would always be quite few in number. I knew that H.B. Boutwell and my sister, Mary, loved me, but never take for granted what a mother and father mean to a young child. They cannot be replaced.

I guess Dad never got over being alone. He tried to keep busy with his business and farm life but that just moved him further from me. My Dad was old when I came along. I never remember him playing with me. There was little time to hunt and fish with him or be like other boys my age. When I was eleven, the Great Depression was forcing the Deep South to slow to a halt as if locked in the dog days of the sweltering August sun. Dad lost his cotton crop because of a small boll weevil that would climb into the red and white cotton bolls and eat the bloom that used to turn those red clay fields into a snow-white September Christmas.

When the crops failed, Dad broke down completely and all we could do was watch the Depression deepen. Even when people started saying the Depression was over, Dad was too ill to recover any part of his former self.

A Great Turn of Events

Early on, well before the Depression, Dad had injured himself and was unable to walk except with the use of two canes. Next, he had a heart attack and took to his bed. No matter what the doctors did, I remember he moaned with pain and could not breathe. He was sent to bed to wait until another attack took his life.

Around the same time, a new type of doctor moved into our town and Dad, who liked new things and new ideas, was not afraid to try him. Within four hours after the first adjustment, Dad could breathe easily and in four days he was out walking around on the farm. No one knew anything about this type of doctor, but I saw how Dad responded and there is no argument about results. This started me thinking about chiropractic.

Soon after, my teacher assigned the class to write a thesis in English class about what we wanted to do after high school. I was impressed with this chiropractor so I wrote something about helping people get better. My teacher liked me. After reading my essay, Miss Beatty told me she had had a positive experience with chiropractic herself and she encouraged me to follow the natural instinct she felt I had to help other people.

Not only did Dad recover, but his last act as a responsible

person was to beg his family to give me the $500 tuition to send me to Davenport, Iowa and Palmer College of Chiropractic.

I paid back the loan in full but just as I completed my first year at Palmer, on a cold, dark rainy day, I was called to Dean Hender's office and told my Dad had passed away. I would have to leave Davenport for a year and try to salvage what Dad did for me. After working at home and saving all I could, I returned to Palmer to finish my degree.

Working two jobs after school kept my head above water but I remember those cold Davenport winters and how little heat and food I had. The last thing Dad did for me that first year was to pick pecans (pee – cons to us southerners) up off the ground from his trees and mail them up to me. I repackaged them and sold them to all my classmates, teachers and everyone else who would soon fall in love with that sweet southern nut. I remember one instructor calling me the "nut man." I took it as a compliment. It meant I was producing and that I had value.

Yes, I was psychologically stunted from my childhood. Psychologists would tell me later I was paranoid about my loved ones leaving me and that I had a fear of getting close to anyone. The Boutwells were not my problem; it was the loss of my Mom and Dad. My sister, along with the Boutwells, did all they could for me and I grew up in their loving home with my nephews. But later, with my own family and fatherhood, it did not seem that I could give myself to anything but my work.

I met my wife Jo in the x-ray labs at Palmer and I had to earn her respect. I can still hear her telling people I did the work of three normal people. But I was not normal. I could have been more intimate, but it was hard. I kept everything inside and held everyone just a little bit away from me. But marrying Jo was the best thing I ever did in my life. Jo was a Godsend and our children, Tom and Beverly, made life worth living. I wish I had been a better husband and father. Maybe every man feels this way, but I really mean it. It was no excuse that I was so busy bringing chiropractic to the world. I know I could have put in more time at home and been closer to these kids. I loved them with my meager love and have always been very proud of them, but regrets are regrets.

When I graduated from Palmer and got back to Georgia, I finally had the courage to call Jo and propose marriage. I was working in the Paulk clinic in Atlanta and I was on the radio but I was still driving an old car and had a poverty attitude, always trying to save my money. When we got married, I thought we did not have the money to go anywhere for our honeymoon so I suggested we drive over to our old home place in Alabama.

The old farmhouse had not been lived in for awhile, but it was just like Dad left it. What I did not know was that my brother J.T. or "Bub" got there before us and hid his car in the barn. Jo brought sheets and pillows and our picnic spread for the night. When we got in bed, Bub jumped out of the big armoire and scared us to death!

Jo really kept me going. I had this fear she might leave me someday. She was always faithful to me and the family, but I had deep fears. I remember when we got our first king-sized bed. I woke up on one of those first nights and Jo was not next to me. I went around the house in a daze waking up my son Tom and bemoaning the loss. We found Jo sound asleep on the other side of that big bed. Tom still likes to tell that story on me.

When Jo died, my life was altered. I could only keep going by making my practice into a refuge. Concentrating on my patients during the day helped a lot. But those long nights and that big bed really got to me. I never got over being alone without my Jo. I guess I am showing my age now, as every time I think about her or talk about her, the tears start rolling down my cheeks.

Jo believed in me at first sight. I did not know that she was the one who persuaded the boss to hire me in the Palmer x-ray lab (Jo was smart too). I got to be in charge of the lab and the techs, including Jo! It was very important to me to have that encouragement and to see someone else felt I could handle the job.

Speaking of getting encouragement, it was my high school English teacher who first accepted me and believed in me before she knew who I really was. Miss Beatty loved me. She was more than just a great teacher. She really saw something worthwhile in me. She talked to me as if I had more talent and possibilities than any other student she had ever taught. The truth is, she probably put her encouragement talents into a lot of students. But, she never had one who needed it more than I did. When I became successful, I kept up with her and thanked her for all she did for me. I remember writing my last note to her on her 104th birthday. Just think how many great years I had to thank her and praise her for all she did for me.

I used this same idea when congratulating my doctors. I would write their mothers and brag about them, telling them about this great doctor son or daughter of theirs. This went a long way, well past praising the doctors themselves. Yes, I can still feel the warm feeling inside me when I think of Miss Beatty. She picked out my talents and let me know that she and God expected great things from me. I dare say that I would know unconditional love from her as if from God himself. I would eventually go to the altar of the Baptist church in Albany, Georgia and give myself to my Lord and Savior Jesus Christ, but Miss Beatty and my wife Jo were the only other human beings who ever believed in me and accepted me with such unconditional love.

God uses other people. I am convinced of this fact more and more all the time. Never forget who stuck with you and believed in you along the way, maybe when you did not believe in yourself. If these people are still alive today, call or write to tell them what they mean to you. Let the truth be known. Make your life like these special encouragers. Look for someone to believe in and encourage today. It seems funny now to believe that I had this talent of encouraging people. Yes, you can be used by God to inspire and motivate others too — it has been one of my most satisfying reasons for being.

IV

Enthusiasm is the Yeast that Raises the Dough

Why is it doctors so often want to tell me about the patient who did not respond, or who made them negative? I kept my head down in practice and listened to those who believed in me who got fantastic results and who would let me be their doctor.

I did not concentrate on what the medical world had going on around me. That was all different than anything I believed in or was teaching. I never ran down medical doctors, but some of them sure made me want to. Not one of them was impressed with my results. Only I and my patients could appreciate chiropractic healing. Back then, MDs believed they were next to the Almighty and that if any patient showed faith in chiropractic, they would let them know we were not *real* doctors.

They would paint us with negative colors by saying we did not have the research to back up our science. That is one reason I am so interested in donating to chiropractic research. Biomechanics is just as complex as our chemistry, and I'm going to put my money into this research, looking more deeply into the subluxation. Somewhere I read we have 70 full-time researchers in chiropractic. I've also read where one drug company has 10,000 researchers looking for new chemicals everyday. We've got to get going! We have to be very positive on our results.

Still, some doctors argue that clinical results (positive anecdotal evidence) need not enter into our treatment plans or even into the profession in general. Don't they know how awful this negative attitude can be? If this attitude and teaching had been around during the past 100-plus years, we would have no chiropractic. I find that ultra-successful chiropractors have full faith in our healing philosophy and teach these wellness concepts to their patients. We have to offer positive hope to patients. We must be firm on our results and principles that explain the anecdotal evidence of our success in helping patients.

Here is some good advice: teach healing, not treatments for symptoms. Keep telling every new patient about your "patient of the month." Keep giving them successful patient testimonials to look over. This gives each patient some of our Big Idea in chiropractic — the power that made the body heals the body and your adjustment releases this power! Or, the body is always changing and the adjustment helps it change for the better over time.

What to watch for

When I was coaching doctors who were not moving ahead in their practices, I heard one common undercurrent in all of their conversations. They were not aggressive with patient care plans. They did not teach that it took time and repetition for innate to change the body. They did not teach chiropractic principles of healing and, in general, acted as if they were embarrassed presenting BIG chiropractic. It made me think they did not believe in chiropractic with all their hearts. In fact, these are the doctors who wanted to tell me mainly about the one patient who did not respond to their adjustments.

Somewhere along the line, these doctors had diluted their science and their own hopes and dreams; many told me they had more faith in chiropractic *before* they went to chiropractic college. I don't know how this could be. Every patient I helped increased my faith. Most of these doctors had this standoffish attitude of fear and doubt. Their attitudes told me that they doubted everything. They spoke of doubting their adjustment, doubting their location, doubting their decision to even become chiropractors. It was this lack of belief I had to erase from their attitudes.

I had to detonate those negative, hazy clouds moving across their minds. What about the next patient who had a great response to their adjustment? Live in that glow of healing! But no, all they could concentrate on was a patient who had not responded the way they had hoped.

I can tell you how the medics are trained. Back in the 1960s, spine surgeons operated on almost every patient with back pain who came into their offices. Of course, they had medical objective indication. But today most MRIs reveal herniated discs in patients with back pain but it doesn't mean the physician performs surgery. Patients need chiropractic first. These old surgeons did laminectomies on nine out of ten backs. Most patients did not improve, got worse, and often went back for multiple surgeries, sometimes even having vertebrae fused.

How did these surgeons feel about their work? Fine! That is what they were taught in medical school and from peers in residency. As time went on, these surgeons changed their teaching. They started bringing conservative spinal care forward so now this same surgeon today operates on far fewer low backs. They all still go on with their practices with full faith in their system and teaching.

Then why can't chiropractors go on basking in their results? I have never heard of a DC crippling a patient, but I have had way too many patients where failed back surgery did just that! Some chiropractors act like they must get 100 percent positive results or they are failures or, worse yet, that patients won't like them. My teaching has always been to look for objective changes. Learn to be thankful when innate heals your patients. If results are not fast enough, send them to doctors with another technique. Don't give up or act like you must have the full answer for every patient. Plus, **get more excited about your results!** This draws patients into your office. I know there are many more satisfied patients to put your power of positive thinking to work. So, Do It!

Learn from your past, but live in the future

I came from a childhood full of disappointment and discouragement. That's the part I had to lick to go forward in my life. I think this is my calling — to show the doctors who struggle from lack of love and support that their problems could be used in their favor if they act in a positive manner. They have to act *as if* they are as good as any doctor and better than most. This helps clinical outcomes to be more positive. Chaos and discouragement make many give up and accept negativity. I found that almost every person has some chaos and discouragement in his life. It's a given. It was always that big part of life that God and I had to lick! "Stinkin thinking," someone called it, will kill you dead in your mission and your healing work.

Write this down and tattoo it on your brain: You must rely on your education and positive outcomes that explain the great results from your adjustments. Expect the best, work hard in full faith for the best, and be prepared for the worst. In all cases, if there is a subluxation, your adjustment will be needed. This may not be the only need, but it is a very important need. Never give up on this point!

If I emphasized anything with the doctors I coached, it was that they can control their own future. Their faith and family should come first, but then it must be full faith in chiropractic. I found if I could get them to control their intensity to carry out the mission I gave them (the "Do It" list), positive things began to happen. Enthusiasm was missing in almost every negative doctor I coached. If belief in their work increased, then enthusiasm increased.

I had doctors write down every patient who responded to care. When a new patient came in, they could take these cases out and show the new person what to expect. I demanded a "Do It" attitude in this pursuit. Don't question, just Do It. All coaches follow this same formula: set goals, set the plan in action, and have the right attitude to Do It!

Sometimes, the enthusiasm does not come around until

doctors begin to see the results of their labor. Some just don't think they can really do it. But they can! Let's look at how we used to map out our seminar goals for every doctor:

Dedication

We want all our doctors to understand the philosophy, healing principles, and intent of chiropractic for all their patients. They must be rock solid on why they are chiropractors, and what part our science must play in the area of healing. Their mission has be one of going the extra mile to prove that innate can heal the patient after the adjustment.

The team effort

The doctor and staff make up the team. The staff meetings, as well as the goal setting and planning, must be a group effort. This unity causes the office and its mission to come together as never before.

Service

Every patient must think he or she has been treated better at your office than at any doctor's office before. They must feel a genuine love and concern. Everyone must get more service than they paid for.

Discipline

The doctor and CAs must be organized and headed down the right path to success. Office systems/staff meetings must be up to total efficiency and there must be this success discipline to carry on day after day.

Enthusiasm

I've already covered this, but know that a team committed to achieve a goal with enthusiasm is a team that will succeed.

Rewards

Every doctor and staff member must profit share and have vacations, time off, perks and pats on the back when the goals are met. Everyone appreciates being appreciated.

Never fail in your mission

Everyone involved in the office must stretch and grow to reach goals that seem out of reach. You must never give up. Never accept defeat and expect to achieve your goals.

The doctor is chief

The doctor must shoulder the responsibility to lead the team and guide the office in the right direction. You cannot delegate this leadership to anyone else. It is a commitment to being in charge that must never waver.

Surround yourself with people who lift you up and bring enthusiasm to everything you do.

V

To Do Good and Help People

I remember living with my sister when I was thirteen years old. The Boutwells loved me and always treated me like family. However, when their own children came along, although I did not feel I was in their way, I just always had this feeling of being alone, and that I must move on. I felt a calling inside of me and a knowledge that soon I would be on my own again.

I know what orphans feel deep inside of them. Although I never felt neglected, I knew my future was up to me and the good Lord. I slept in a room away from everyone, unheated and cold in winter. It was on one of those cold winter nights I got down on my knees and prayed.

Help me, God, to do good and help people.

The first time I prayed that prayer it startled me because I had no direction in life. Somewhere within me, though, there was this inner urge to do good and help people. I started saying this prayer every night over and over. It became me. I became it. Many years later, as a young doctor, I was still praying this prayer. It was my "breath prayer." It was my theme song. It is truly my vow given to me by God. It was my door to open, so to speak, a way for God to use me in this life.

In practice, this prayer propelled me into a dynamic, re-volving door of service. All I could give, I gave. Patients picked up on this inner desire to help them more than any doctor ever had before. I became a magnet to sick people. I could tell what my patients were going to say even before they said it. Even today, I still get glimpses of my input into someone's life and, almost immediately, I call them and ex-press my thoughts to them. Usually they tell me my words came at the right time. It is still this divine inspiration I seek today.

I think God keeps me around to help people. I keep a pen and paper ready to write down the next inspiration, like BJ's "flash thots" he said came to him from innate. These inspira-tions are still a great lever in my life today. I knew when I said this first prayer that it was never said to make a lot of money. Money was a sequel to the prayer, combined with determined actions. No, I think I was praying for direction, support and a glimpse into the unknown, into my future. Even today, when I have a blue day and I can't seem to get motivated, I pray this little prayer. I look for the unknown to come into my mind and soothe my anger, my anticipation and my haughtiness.

I'm old enough now to know death will come. I tell eve-ryone, when I am 103 years old I'll get shot by a jealous man chasing me down the street because his girlfriend is at-tracted to me and my good looks. Ha! Seriously, I am not afraid to die. I have outlived almost all my enemies. I have watched people die. When I was first in practice all doctors made house calls. I had patients who had more faith in me than they did in another trip to the hospital. They would call me to their death beds.

I would give them adjustments and, almost always, they would smile, squeeze my hand and thank me for my efforts. I wanted to do more, but it was a reminder of my own mor-tality. There were no Emergency Rooms or the life support technology we know today. People were allowed to die at home. I don't know what to think about doctors who pride themselves today on their ability to keep patients alive be-yond the patient's own capability to return to some quality of life. I don't want that for me, but there is that training in society to put the end of your life in medical hands. I think that is always the chiropractor's nightmare, don't you?

I know there is much good in this technology; it's sometimes necessary but has little to do with health. I see them bring back young people from trauma. It is right if they can bring them back to some quality of life. But for the elderly, whose major systems are destroyed or shut down, I say, "Let us die."

I watched my wife, Jo, die a slow, painful death. It was heartbreaking. I can just imagine how devastating it must be for parents to lose a child. Thank God we never had to go through that. What I want to say here about dying is a salient point. Life is not about dying. It is about how much you can do for people today and how you live your life today. I used to teach Sunday school and I remember the Apostle Paul's positive letters to his churches. He was encouraging them to run their race in life with endurance. He wanted them all to bloom where they were planted. It is integrity that counts. This involves bearing fruit from honesty, happiness, joy and love.

Even when others don't treat you right you must still keep on treating others right, with the same love and appreciation you want to be treated with yourself. You can never out-give the giver. You can never get ahead in your attitude with living your life in yesterdays or tomorrow. You have to start on today, doing what needs to be done, even though you may not want to do it. Maybe it is something uncomfortable, like spinal screenings. I think we have to do uncomfortable things to appreciate when comforts come.

Those first struggling years in practice bonded Jo and me together more than anything else. They always gave us "look back" conversations to smile about. Ask yourself how much you want to help people. How much time and energy do you have to put into someone's life? I was always jealous of my wife and how she could love better than I, how she could focus everything on the children and grandchildren. She would bend over backwards to find the next exciting thing to do with these kids. I was bored with a lot of things the family did. It is my fault of course. I had the wrong attitude, or I was thinking of my business or something else that kept me from focusing on the moment with them.

It hurt me that I could not completely suppress this cold part of me. I think it's vital for young men to focus on being better spouses and parents. It was hard for me, but I see a lot of great parents out there today. My problem was just me and my attitude. I thought I had to accomplish earth-shattering deeds; things that would make me another million. I was interested in my interests. My wife Jo could be interested in these little kids' interests. She said she was building memories. I did not know what she was talking about. Now I know, but it's too late.

This is good advice for you doctor. Listen up! Looking back with the perfect science of hindsight, I could have changed my attitude to spend more time with the family. I could have chosen to see their lives and activities as more important than mine. I know I would have received greater blessings, because now most of their memories are about their Mom and Grandma, not me.

Maybe it is this provider gene that kept me on my own agenda. I need an excuse you see. No, I think I just had a selfish attitude. I really wanted to do my thing the most. Now, I wish I had focused in on their "little" things. My loss! I think every father, if he is not drawn to share in his children's lives, should learn how to take the time to be in their lives. I never talked to a doctor ever who said he wished he would have spent more time at the office and less time with the children. So, think about making those memories and make them BIG!

Today, have that conference with your creator. Go into your spiritual self and ask about your future and the present things that concern you. Listen for ideas and answers and go for it. Remember the principle I taught you about testing the answers that come through. If it is from God, it cannot hurt someone, cannot be immoral, and it must agree with divine viewpoint (the Holy Bible). That is what I see as the standard when judging your actions or "thot flashes."

Someone once said, "God may wait but He is never late." Keep asking how you can serve more and work like heck where you are now! Ask God to show you how you can be of more value to your family, friends and patients. Ask how you can do more with less complaining. Ask. Ask and it will come. I'm not preaching here. I am not a Bible scholar, but I know most of the commands and truths in the Bible and I feel they are from God.

There is nothing new under the sun. All knowledge and truth is to be gained. All knowledge started out with a mystery. But no knowledge started out as magic. You can't wish your life was different. You have to go to work with what you have today. You have to be tenacious. You have to understand the rules, work the rules and never quit. Remember my first words at my seminar, "Success can be learned: I expect you to learn it here!" Even if success comes later, instead of sooner, never give up on your dreams.

Keep striving toward your dreams and looking every day for ways you can help others as you pursue them.

VI

Attitude Means Everything in Life

When I ran personality profiles on my doctors I found some were so laid back they took motivation the wrong way. Others had to have every fact at hand and were analytical to the point of inactivity. Insights from personality testing helped me show them where their strengths were, how they were wired, and what they needed to focus on to move the practice to the next level.

We are all combinations of various personality types. The key is to identify which is the dominant personality and which traits we need to further cultivate to become more well rounded. Here is one way of looking at dominant personality types.

The Drivers
Lions roaring in the jungle

There are many ways to picture this type of person. They are absolutely driven to succeed. It does not mean they are wise business people, but they have a lot of initiative to work with. I am one of them.

In his book, *The Two Sides of Love*, Gary Smalley paired animals with certain personality types. This book is a must-read for you. He called the drivers lions. They often don't do a whole lot more than roar in the jungle but they look fearsome and fear nothing.

These lion doctors roar up the mountainside to success,

but also often make the biggest mistakes and fall farthest and hardest. All doctors need some lion within them. If you are timid or afraid, learn to roar! When you make a decision, "Do It" no matter what! Be willing to stick your head through the wall!

These doctors are also sometimes stubborn and insensitive. They need to work on being more analytical or "softer." Drivers seem to have a one-track mind to get their goals accomplished. When I see this raw trait in a new doctor, I have no trouble increasing his or her practice because these doctors want to make good more than anything. They will do the things I say to do. The only exception was the drivers who were just out of college and thought they knew everything. After they tasted the real world and their unproven ideas didn't pan out, they would become coachable.

Drivers dominate people. They also have a lot of rough edges to polish to get them to shine in the right areas. It will be a lifetime effort, but like all changes for the better, it is worth the effort. Drivers can get sidetracked or involved in too many areas. They need one track to achieve. You see, a driver can think about fishing so much that he gets on the front page of *Bass Fishing* magazine but still have a luke- warm practice. He needs direction to focus his drive.

I have watched this type of doctor concentrate so much on making money that he or she forgets honesty, the profes- sion in general, and even the patients. These are the ones who are red flagged for billing at the top range. These are the doctors whose attitude is to "Do It," but who sometimes want to cut corners to find a way. Drivers are risk takers and sometimes need to be more prudent in their decision mak- ing.

Find a way to be driven. You want to develop this type of personality trait because you are in business for yourself. Give me ten of these doctors over the pessimists or the doc- tors who want to gather information but refuse to act until all the facts are known or until it suits them.

Lions also sometimes begin to believe they cannot fail.

Pride gets them out of touch with God and everyone else. Luckily, they tend to mellow with age and begin to realize the importance of relationships. But, in the meantime, they can make hasty investment decisions, put too little stock in the value of their families and engage in questionable ethics. Although everyone who is in business for himself needs to cultivate some traits of the driven lion, all thoughts and actions should be run through these three filters:

1. Will my actions or choice hurt anyone?
2. Is it morally and ethically right?
3. Does it agree with God's standards and guidelines?

The Analytical
Busy beavers

These doctors spend all night reading the instruction manuals on their new computers and like it! They are busy beavers but also want to check every angle of a situation before making a decision. Sometimes, they become full-time information gatherers unwilling to finally decide and act, always assuming the most pessimistic outcome if they do or being dissatisfied with any results less than perfection. They like to think they are being realistic — as if those of us who are successful are unrealistic.

I was perplexed at first how to help this type doctor but soon learned that the key was to believe in them with all my heart until they could finally believe in themselves. They also need to hone in on their most positive strength and build on that. I could find that positive strength to work with in everyone. I prayed about this. Remember my prayer every night for ever and ever was:

Lord, let me do good and help people.

This was also my daily prayer when I was in practice. I worked hard to find some way to excite the doctors I was coaching. Usually this happened when they saw they could increase their service and their incomes. When they started rolling and their numbers were climbing, I saw changes I never expected. I was always waiting for the time when they looked at me and spoke to me as if they knew a lot more than I did. That was when they usually wanted to leave. However, like all the doctors who I helped, these doctors eventually came to me with thankfulness and gratitude for my help at a time when they most needed it.

Beavers like to tell me they "just want to do it right." It is true that the lions don't mind failing a little, picking up and moving ahead, but this kills the analytical person. I had to convince them that you can't be accurate with every shot. You are going to miss the mark sometimes. This type of person needs to learn to risk, expect to fall a bit, and learn they can recover and go on in life. I had to take it slow and easy with these types of doctors, encouraging them to risk and to reward their failures. Just like the lion personality needs more beaver in them, the beaver needs more lion thinking.

Happy-go-Lucky Pleasure Seeker
Playful otters

These doctors tripped me up most in coaching. They are so good at motivation, speaking and wooing you into their way of thinking, you forget they are like houses made of papier mâché. They smile and boost you up, but they can never seem to get to the goals. They want to think you can succeed by just going along.

They need to concentrate on the business side of practice (patient relationships come easily to them) so I focused on teaching them discipline. They tend to want to practice two or three days a week and brag the rest of the time. When you hear them give a speech, you would think they had the best practices in the world, only to find out later they had never made it to second base. These are the otters. They are fun-loving animals but not too serious about work and setting goals.

The most successful approach with these doctors turned out to be getting them to set a goal, work with it long enough to accomplish it, and then set the next goal. These doctors were my friends for life. They clung to me and networked with me for my business like no one else. They were tough to get solid for the long haul, but when they did, they were great successes. I had to work with their strengths and this was the key. A person who works on his or her weaknesses throughout life dies with strong weaknesses. My job was to find their strengths and get them to lean on these positive points and use them to move forward in practice.

Mama's Boy
The pleasing golden retrievers

These doctors came to me after Mama had gone on to live in heaven; she wouldn't let him or her succeed while she was still busy providing her care. I am exaggerating, but this type of doctor is so loyal and has such a fierce desire to please people, he or she often can't take the leadership role at home or in the office. These are the compassionate doctors who would do anything for their patients. I knew a young doctor once who told me he had to give up a successful practice because he took the patients' pain and suffering home at night and it worried him too much. His uncontrolled passion for these patients was making him symptomatic. This is too much of a soft side. The golden retriever needs to do more than just develop his tougher side, he has to get that look off his face that says, "I'll do whatever you want." The golden retriever needs more beaver and more lion personality.

They already have the compassion and love, but they also need to learn to take charge and to not always believe everything they are told. It is hard to encourage them to offer adjustment plans because they want to avoid rejection at all cost. It helped them when I developed for them a list of adjustment plans a patient could choose from. They want to avoid rejection at any cost.

After you read Gary Smalley's book, you will see you genetically have tendencies toward a certain personality type and lifestyle, but that you can integrate pieces of the various traits into your personality through personal reflection, studying the other types and taking direction from a coach.

The attitude you choose to bring to your practice and to your life will do much to determine how far you go.

VII

Change Their Teaching
Change the Profession
Change the World

There was a time when I believed all I had to do was be like BJ; get the atlas adjusted and everyone's ailments would go away. That reminds me, I must go to Roy Sweat's office today and get my atlas adjusted. I owe special thanks to Dr. Sweat, Dr. Amodio and all the chiropractors who look after me today. I no longer believe BJ had all the answers, but I've never forgotten the value of having my atlas and axis clear.

I think the strength of BJ's "adjust the atlas/axis only" was to have one central thought for patients to grasp. That theme created great interest in my mission and purpose in Albany, Georgia. I went from BJ "HIO" toggle to Grostic adjusting and then, finally, to full spine and modalities to help patients get over acute pain. I worked hard to have that "something special" in my adjustment that BJ always kept talking about. I never bought into all that straight-mixer controversy. I did not like politics and tried to stay out of it.

Having modalities in your office to help patients in acute pain is fine with me, but you still have to be a great adjuster. The politics of straight or mixer caused more conflict than good and that made me scared to be involved in policy making at all. Instead, I worked hard helping all those doctors I coached who came from other colleges. They didn't need me to comment on their treatment philosophy and scope of practice, but they did need me to help them focus on one specific point in their healing mission.

I helped them place strong emphasis on the "special adjustment" for each patient. When they mostly had medical concepts and wanted acceptance like MDs, I did not discourage this high priority. But, they did not have hospital access and I had to show them where this would leave them short. With no drugs, no hospital support and little worldly respect, they had to have a different attitude. I took the way they had been taught and believed and grounded them in the greatness of chiropractic, like BJ did for me.

I found that chiropractors, as a whole, are really caring and wonderful doctors. All I had to do was show them that they also had more than an adjusting or healing purpose. They had to have a plan to teach the greatness of chiropractic. This was more important to the growth of their practices than helping the patients get over their conditions. Patients started getting better results in their offices and their practices grew after this coaching. I could see more potential in them than they could see in themselves.

I liked taking on the doctors no other consultant wanted. Many of these doctors practiced on the back roads in their states. I found out how to help them raise their profile. When they started to assert themselves, I could feel their power.

As I said, I don't believe everyone has to be a rabid straight doctor like BJ wanted. I never taught being straight and I believed it was a detriment to teach that this was the only way to practice. Everyone is different and schools teach different concepts. We need to forget the politics. I could see that these doctors had been trained to have faith in their modalities and that is good. It was not up to me to change this thinking. I was careful not to degrade their colleges and training.

That straight/mixer stuff was about building political camps. It was not important to helping doctors succeed. So listen to this you "technique heads" because this is very important. You don't get unity with degradation, just like you don't get positive change by criticism. My emphasis was on giving them my hope, my faith and belief that they could be more than they thought they could be and that chiropractic was more than treatments for pain. I saw doctors who believed they were mediocre go on to great success and service to sick people. Many of these doctors found success a great elixir and their heads and bellies would swell up with pride. Others were like those of us who went through the Depression; thankful for every step forward and ever mindful of the meager times of yesterday.

I have just one regret about my doctors; there were too many divorces. It is true that many of the husbands and wives from the early years could not stand the prominence of success later on. I know many husbands started looking around for new wives once they became successful (and vice versa). In all honesty, I do not know what really caused the high incidence of divorces in my client base except to say that it followed the divorce trend and rates of our nation as a whole. I hate to think that their new success in practice was a contributing factor. Maybe it was the times, the popularity of divorce, or the way of the world? Broken families hurt me deeply, but that's another story.

At Practice Consultants (PC), Dee Warren and I had four classes going at once. Every other month, a new class of doctors, CAs and spouses came to our meetings. We taught them a direct plan for each month. They had to accomplish their goals. I motivated them to stretch and grow. My monetary success came from a percentage of the doctor's increased income. Many doctors got so big under my tutelage that they disliked writing those large checks to PC every month. However, many others were very thankful and compliant.

My claim to fame was that I decided to put all the profits in a foundation (the Foundation for the Advancement of Chiropractic Education) as my other investments kept me from ever having to take a salary from PC. The Foundation was my vehicle for helping the profession. It was because of what I learned as a coach and the fact that our teaching changed so many lives that I got excited thinking about the day when I could turn my full interest toward changing our chiropractic profession and helping students and colleges succeed. There would come a day that I could command respect and change things with this money.

I want to see unity in chiropractic. Dave Palmer put me on this mission and since he has been gone, I am carrying on for him. I can't remember just when I decided to donate to these other colleges. I helped Dave create the ACA in the sixties. When BJ died in 1962, Dave took over Palmer College and made me the first alumni president. I even got BJ and Dave together in Sarasota when BJ was on his death bed. God used me to help reconcile father and son. Later, I helped Dave with his ICA/ACA unity plans. If Dave could have gotten the ICA to join with the ACA, there's no telling where we would be today. If you're up there listening Dave, I still believe in unity. I won't give up your dream, Dave, that we can one day unite and that our colleges can create a unified emphasis that will get this big job done.

I was trying to set a course of giving to colleges. When I investigated our educational institutions, I found varied philosophies as well as misunderstood goals and missions. Many colleges did not even teach the chiropractic principles of our founders. Some were homeopathic colleges that had changed their name to include chiropractic. But what drew me to other colleges was the fact that they needed help. Some were having great difficulties because they were not using sound business principles and practices. I think God gave me the gift to spot poor business practices because I have helped so many colleges in trouble. Other colleges convinced me they needed research money. God knows, we need that.

One of my first efforts was to put a million dollars into National College's research. I was new at donating and I made the mistake of not specifying how it was to be spent. This was a big mistake, and one that made me more careful later. I started specifying that colleges had to match the grant. I began to teach them how to raise money. Plus, the money had to be spent as I directed.

My next grant was to Texas Chiropractic College because they had a very small enrollment at the time and they needed money and students. I helped them with both. I had an old friend who I went to Palmer with (Dr. Wolfe) who was the president of Northwestern College and I gave to his college as a friend. It was fun. It felt like Christmas! We named my building the Wolfe/Harris building. It was sort of like setting up my doctors in small towns. I wanted them to make a big splash in a small pond.

At some colleges, I set up a practice management teaching endowed chair. My purpose was to get them to teach my success system. I found out that our schools taught very little practice management.

I was never really upset over calling our adjustments "manipulation" or "treating subluxations." That never bothered me because truth will always come around and it was my goal to see chiropractic claim its solid place as the most researched and practiced adjusting science in the world. I think time will prove me out. Because every doctor who has made it his life's long work to study the subluxation complex knows we are only scratching the surface in our research and understanding of this entity. There is a place in every college to teach natural modalities and other regimens targeted at symptoms/conditions and this is good. However, we must also research and teach the value of and the skill needed to adjust the spine and extremities. The adjustment is a billion dollar idea! Never forget I said this.

I never got into techniques or treatments for conditions with my clients but I taught why adjusting works! Here is the key: I fed off of the positive results in my practice for my proof. I focused on results and related those healing stories to patients. That is, after all, what got chiropractic to where it is today. We don't have all the answers (no one does), but new testing and new technologies are here and more are coming that will help us adjust better and prove our results.

Let's teach this to patients in full faith. Some doctors hate to hear faith related to chiropractic practice, but I can't back up every cured case with published papers and double blind studies. I know we have to be scientific but, believe me, medicine can't back up everything it does and can't even explain all the many side effects of so many of its procedures What I say is that we need the same intensity on teaching and researching chiropractic as they have about finding new drugs.

I see the day coming where our research will burrow more deeply into the neuromechanical mechanism affected by the adjustment. This is why I support Chris Colloca and his research. This will aim us more toward specific adjusting as our clinical focus. What if a national campaign stimulated people to have their spine tested and adjusted? This will come when that value has been instilled as a need in people lives (like it is with us). I say, "Chiropractors are the future health doctors." This must be the thrust, because it will be our future.

I see us working with all doctors. I see us adjusting in every facility, not just hospitals. Maybe there is a good message here that all doctors have the same amount of basic science and practice equality and that we can all interact and get along together. The goal has to change to the needs of the patient first. I look forward to the day when the subluxation will be the big breakthrough on the six o'clock news and every doctor and hospital will demand adjustments for all their patients. The body heals better and faster with adjustment. But we must not lose our identity or the founding principles of our profession. In my mind, I am helping every college to go back to the greatness in chiropractic by teaching pride and faith in our great science.

My first goal as a clinician was to see how much good my adjustments did for the patient and how much change the patient could make with just this treatment (adjustment) first. It never ceased to amaze me that, after adjustments only, the patient's entire life could change. If you focus on innate curing the patient, you set your practice into a lifetime service for patients. I went on and on with my patients their first two weeks about the adjustment and what it was doing. After about two weeks, I could see where other treatments were needed, but my plan was to leave the adjustment firmly planted in the patient's mind and body.

I was so insistent I knew when they were subluxation free, or as stable as possible, that this intent created inside of me a super clinician's attitude. I visualized myself as the best doctor for each patient. I really believed a patient could stay with me for life and need very little medical care except for trauma. Sometimes they might need drugs due to years of dysfunction from not being adjusted, but I wasn't negative about that.

I became like a magnet, drawing patients to my large, successful practice. Call it my one- track mind, but I was determined that if the patients stayed with me long enough to clear out, their lives would change and they would see the benefit to keeping checked and adjusted for their entire lives, like we do. It was this attitude in practice that generated power in my life and practice because I was on a mission to clear out patients. I saw this attitude in all the chiropractic greats: BJ, Grostic, Gonstead, Thompson, Goodheart, DeJarnette, Toftness, Van Rumpt, Sweat, Pettibon, and every successful chiropractic great I have ever known. To all of us, correcting subluxations was a bigger idea than drugs, bigger than the propaganda of the medical media, bigger than most of what everyone else knew.

A lot is known about sickness, but we are the ones who look at health, normal function and the innate intelligence inside. This is what I was about and what chiropractic is about. This is what I believe my patients were drawn to. Now, I am about getting this positive success attitude taught in all our colleges. I have donated extensively to six chiropractic colleges. I intend to put my money and influence in every student I can before and after my time on earth.

My big push in 2003 was to help fund the new research building at Palmer. It is here that all the government money for research is funneled. With this fast-moving technology age we can work together more efficiently and move forward like never before. It was believed that the Genome research would take decades to understand. It took ten years to isolate a few chromosomes until someone put them in a computer "blender" and got the families of genes separated. I hope in my lifetime we will have a consortium of all our college research departments and that chiropractic will be understood and moving forward much like the Genome research. When that happens — look out!

Understanding the adjustment will spread like wild fire running through the colleges, the profession and the world. That is why we want to be known first and foremost from our donations in this area. There can still be a place for nutrition, acupuncture, PT, mind control, etc. These things have their place and some doctors are more interested in this than adjusting. That is fine with me. There is room for all types of natural healing with our science. The research will sort it out and I believe the adjustment still does the most good. We are the experts in this field and we need to hang on to this status.

Do what you do best, doctor, and keep working to improve this service.

VIII

Ms. Dee Warren

I want to devote time and space here to praise my able assistant, Dee Warren. I was busy in Albany when she came into me for blinding headaches and depression. She had been everywhere with no relief. However, when I got her atlas cleared out, she became a new person.

Dee was one of those really grateful patients. You know, some patients think just because they paid the office fee that they deserve to get well. Dee was different and wanted to do something for chiropractic. She was one of those who could not tell enough people about the wonders of chiropractic. Miracles happen after adjustments. She was the proof.

As I said many times, adjustments restore life and health to sick people. One day, Ms. Warren (as I always called her) said she had decided to work in chiropractic and asked if I would hire her. She had been working for years in the local yarn mill and had no degrees. I was not hiring at that time, so I said no, but I liked her spirit. On her next visit she told me again how thankful she was that she had finally gone to a chiropractor. Then she reminded me that she had referred all her family and friends to me and that no patient or employee would ever match her number of referrals.

The next time I saw her she would not stop talking about the great value of the adjustments in her life and how she could see herself working in my office. I was pleased, of course, with her praise, but I did not need another CA at that time. After I told her this she said, "I will be working for you and chiropractic some day." I told her to go back to school and take some business courses, thinking that would get her off my case.

Months later, when she came in for her adjustment, she told me that she had the courses and, with her new skills, was ready to start to work for me. I guess I hired her mainly because of her persistence (was it me who said something about determined persistence?). I admire persistence more than talent. Also, perhaps I saw some of my own struggles in this woman. She was a single mother without a lot of money or hope of succeeding, but she had a burning desire to give back to chiropractic. Who was it who said you are never poor when you have something to give?

In the office she stood out as the most excited chiropractic person on staff. Being a CA was not just a job, it was her mission. She referred more patients to me than any other CA who ever worked for me. Plus, she would come to almost every health class I put on for new patients. Sometimes she would fly in my airplane with me to the different clinics I owned. I could see that the CAs in these offices respected her for her dedication.

Speaking of my flying days and my attitude toward money, one day I was coming back from Mississippi where the cost of aviation fuel was high so I took off without enough fuel and figured I'd stop in Alabama or Georgia for more. I ran out of fuel and had to make an emergency landing in a cotton field in Alabama. The money it cost to tow the plane out of the field and the grief from the Federal Aviation Administration taught me a lesson. But my poverty attitude made me want to cut every penny in half.

Back to Dee, when I was ready to start Practice Consultants Seminars, I picked Dee to be my assistant. She was more than willing to do all the work. She had been helping me with my talks anyway and she was tireless in her efforts. Then I told her she had to teach the CA classes. That is when she said her first "No." She just did not believe she could ever talk in front of a large group of people. So, I explained that her salary was going to be tied to the increase in each doctor's income, but that she could not be part of my organization unless she was willing to instruct. That changed her mind.

She became a great teacher. Soon, everyone was bragging on her more than they were on me! I always had this deep southern drawl that most people could not understand, so she worked with me on my diction. I never got much better, but soon she developed her own "radio voice" and would stand next to me on stage asking to piggyback when she knew the audience did not understand what I was teaching. I was furious with these interruptions at first, but soon she got me over myself. We made a great team.

Later, Marilyn Hendrix came on board to help us and soon we were giving as many as 24 seminars a year. I sold my last practice and moved to Atlanta where we could serve full time in this consulting work. I felt gifted by God to help chiropractors. I stayed on the phone all day, everyday, filling up the new classes and consulting with my doctors. It was a great time in my life. I don't miss all the work, because today I could not do this physically, but I miss the thrill of doing a good job, helping so many achieve success, and making so much money.

Every doctor must know there is a peak performance period, so you need to work as hard as you possibly can during those years. Now, you do not want to ignore your family, but there is a relatively small time line of maximum performance that you want to take advantage of in practice. After you go to the mountain top, you will not have to go there again, except in your mind. The fact is, like an Olympic athlete, there are only a couple decades at most when you can keep the intensity at a peak level. The key is to save your income for the days when you slow down.

I tried my best to keep Ms. Warren in my investment scheme. She made a lot of profit in stock that I suggested, but usually she drew it all out to give to her family. After we retired she had a severe auto accident. The trauma left her mind and body disabled. She never recovered. Dementia was in her family too, but she was too young in my book.

Finally, she had to be confined to a nursing home. I still visited her and paid her bills every month. It was sad for me to see my old partner and friend looking at me with a blank stare. We could have shared our old business success together. Sometimes though, you don't get what you want in life.

Goodbye, Dee, may you rest in peace.

IX

Chiropractic Students Listen Up!

I like to speak at our colleges. The energy from the students still excites me. Preparing to speak pulls my youth back to the surface like nothing else these days. I feel the sparks flying in my soul to speak about chiropractic and success.

I lectured at a success seminar the other day and was told I was the highlight of the meeting. It must not have been a very exciting meeting, after all, I am over 85. Who could excite a crowd at 85? I thought I could not give a speech when I was young, but I learned later that indeed I could. Everyone should go to Toastmasters and learn to speak. Many of our colleges have a lecture club; students go to this club and picture yourself telling the chiropractic story to millions of people.

I tell every student that he or she has only 30 to 35 years of productivity as a chiropractor. Maybe I will amend that if I make it to100 and can still give a good talk and clear out an atlas! So, we have to give it all we can when we are young.

Before I go on about what I tell students today, I want to go back to my time at Palmer. In Davenport, my deep southern drawl would not go away. My Yankee classmates made a lot of fun of me. I couldn't change, so I decided to just keep pronouncing my words with double and triple syllables. "Yes," will always be "Ya' ess."

My dad and my high school English teacher encouraged me to be a chiropractor. Dad was left in bed with the shades down after a severe heart attack. The medics in those days recommended no exercise. They said exercise was bad for the heart (of course they were saying this as they lit up another cigarette in their offices). They recommended he stay in bed and stop all activity. A friend of Dad's got him up and took him to the chiropractor, Dr. H.G. Ezell in Birmingham. After his first adjustment, Dad's life changed for the better. He got completely well and never forgot the power of an adjustment.

Later, in school, Ms. Beatty encouraged me to pursue a chiropractic education. I had so little encouragement that I jumped at the chance to go to Iowa, even though I knew nothing about chiropractic nor had I ever had an adjustment myself. Halfway through, I had to go home for a year to work so we would not lose the farm, but I never lost any love or drive to get back to Davenport.

After I graduated from Palmer in 1938, I took a job in the xray department under P.A. Remier. One of the employees in the department was my future wife Jo. I liked teaching her what to do as I was such a great doctor (in my mind) at 23 years old! I also met Dr. Luther Hunter from St. Louis at Lyceum and he offered me a job in his clinic. When I got to St. Louis, he told me that KWTO radio station was in his building and that I would be presenting a five minute radio talk everyday. I was scared, but without time to think of it, I became a radio speaker. I found it was easy talking to a microphone. Soon I was standing in my little booth, orating to the world about the wonders of chiropractic. I learned that the more I talked about our work, the better I understood it myself. You learn by teaching. I got new insights each time I studied and prepared to give a talk.

When I moved to Georgia, I was hired by Dr. Hershel Standford in Atlanta. When he hired me he wanted me to work for nothing. I told him that I was this big radio personality in St Louis and that I would double his practice when I got there. We bargained with spirit, but I got the salary I wanted and headed to Georgia. Also, when I began my own practice, the first thing I did was drive over to the local radio station. Back then no one knew much about our type of doctor. We had a central theme, "Try chiropractic. If you are tired of your aches and pains, if you are told to just keep taking more pills and swallowing more potions, try something new and different. Try chiropractic." All we wanted was for people to try us. We could cure them if we could just break down the fear of the unknown. After hearing me give my lectures to new patients, local chiropractors began coming over every week to my office for me to give them a presentation. Soon I was a coach and didn't know it.

When I opened my office in Albany, Georgia, I knew I had found where God wanted me to be. Everyone kept saying how glad they were that I had come to town. I had started first in McDonough, GA, which is south of Atlanta, but it never felt right. I could not get going in that town. Then I had an opportunity to move to Albany, so I did. I kept my prayer up everyday.

Lord, I am here to help sick people,
help me to be a great doctor.

I kept up my positive self talk. I kept saying to myself, "I will not be average." The harder I worked and the more positive I became the more good I did and the more God blessed me.

The war came on and I was sent my draft notice for a physical. Jo and I had married when I moved back to Georgia but had no children yet. I told my patients I would soon be leaving for the war. I could not visualize myself in the Army, but the draft notices said otherwise. I could see chiropractors in uniform with the chiropractic emblem on their lapel (I still see that today). I kept this vision of myself as a DC commissioned and practicing in the Army. In my heart (self talk) I kept asking God to let me stay home and take care of my patients or, if I had to go, to be that special chiropractor in the Army.

Of course, there was no way I was going to break down the medical barriers in the Army, but in my heart I felt I would not go to war unless I went as a chiropractor. You won't believe what happened. I did not know I had such patients. The town "fathers" were good patients of mine and they and their wives badgered the Draft Board with letters about how much my patients needed me here at home. Some of my patients went in person to the Draft Board meetings to speak on my behalf. Soon, they started in on the President. Even I don't know how this went as far as it did. All I did was put out a tiny "seed thot" like BJ taught me to do.

One day, I got a letter from President Franklin D. Roosevelt himself on White House stationery. It said that I was needed in my city as a chiropractor more than the Army needed me and that I would be exempt from service. Even today, I have a hard time telling this true story. I know that it happened because I visualized in my mind's eye that I somehow would not have to go in the Army. I also visualized that someday chiropractors would wear the officer's uniform. I am living now to see that day too, for our commissioning in the Armed Forces is just a moment away.

Not everything I thought so passionately about and prayed about came true. I prayed for years that those tumors would not take the life of my wife Jo. She was a courageous fighter and we did everything known to science to stop the metastasis. It took me forever to get over her loss. All of my success and all that I have done, Jo was always with me. She knew me when I was nothing. She had more faith in me than I had in myself. Yes, I could visualize what I wanted to happen, but I did not visualize Jo not being with me.

Our two children were mostly grown, and I would be alone for life. I could not will her to live. It was not like being drafted. Experience taught me to seek what was right in a big way. I found there was no power in my visualization when it was not in the will of God. I could not force God, and all my wealth and influence meant little to God. But with Jo? Well, when I get to heaven I will know the rest of that story.

My practice was really big. I was making the big bucks

now. I was on the bank board and on several corporation boards. I invested in real estate and stock and everything seemed to hit for me. Every month I bought shares of AFLAC life insurance stock. I became invincible. And then, I fell flat. For every great mountain you climb, if you do not give thanks to God for the greatness in it, you fall flat. What I found was that God wants nothing from the world but our obedience and thanks. He wants nothing material that we think is important. Money to Him is green paper. No success can supersede His power and your obedience to Him. Something always comes into your life to jerk your chain. It is never *what* but *when*. So, take this to heart: success is what you want, but success is no respecter of persons. Even crooks are successful and even success can be boring. You have to be living in your next vision for your life. You have to be seeing your next goal ahead of you and you have to be moving in the right direction for your life. Some talk about being "in the will of God." I would say that is the only way to move.

In Albany, Georgia, it was the thing to be in an office building with other doctors, but I had the thought of having my own personal clinic on Main Street. I did just this, as well as training more doctors. Then I started opening other clinics all over Georgia. My goal was to get a doctor in there, train him in my system and then let him buy the office from me. I started 15 offices this way in six different states and all were successful. I think this was because I would fly my plane to where the clinics were and personally help my doctors become successful. Then I let them take the credit for their success. I made 50% of their profits and then made money on the sale so I became a practice banker and able to retire by the age of 36.

These retirement years were the most boring two years I ever spent. Life was much more exciting when we first started with nothing and started building our practice. At retirement, all I had to think about was myself and my fortune. I became stale. Jo and the kids were tired of too much Dad. So I went back in practice and started consulting, but that's another story.

I want to say some things to today's chiropractic students:

First, make those special friends. These friendships from chiropractic school will lift you up your entire life. My best friends are all chiropractors. There is no one who knows how you feel about life and changing the world with chiropractic better than these friends.

Next, study as hard as you can. You want to know everything the medics know so become a master of the basic and chiropractic sciences. Get in the lecture clubs and technique clubs. Learn to move the bones in every way known to the profession. Learn to clear out those subluxations. God will lead you to the technique or combination of techniques that is best for you. Don't fret about this too soon. It will all come together in your clinic experience. If it does not, then intern and associate when you graduate and learn from a successful doctor before going out on your own.

Get a job in college. Become so busy that you learn time management at an early age. You must learn to work. Just being in school all your life without any real jobs keeps you in a fantasy world. In the south, pecans were harvested in great quantities and shipped all over the world. My Dad sent me a hundred pounds to sell. I repackaged them and sold them door to door. Soon I was called the "nut boy." I liked how it felt to be my own boss and have people look at me for what I could deliver as a service, instead of just another person existing in the world.

Dr. Galen Price in philosophy class singled me out one day for some nuts and I found that one incident brought more esteem in the eyes of my classmates than what little personality I had.

Finally, I would not marry in college. I know I am on thin ice here these days, getting into gender. I met my wife in Davenport, but I waited until I was out of school for a couple of years before we married. I know everything has changed these days, but my advice on a mate would be to find someone who really believes in you. That is so powerful. Also, you need someone who believes in chiropractic with all his or her heart, like you do, and who wants to raise the children without medical intervention. You need someone who is interested in living the chiropractic lifestyle. This must be a person who wants to put chiropractic across to the world as your marriage team's mission. After God and family, this is more important than houses, cars and country clubs.

Pray to marry someone who wants to be part of something bigger than you. I believe everyone has the right person out there so pray them in! Lastly, after you have made your success in practice, give back to your college and to chiropractic research. We all should give back to that basic learning that enabled us to make our fortunes.

X

It's Not How You Start Off

It's How You End Up

There was a great comedian in my time called Flip Wilson. Flip was one of over a dozen children from a poor family. He said he had no encouragement as a boy, but he had a secret desire in his heart. He fed on that desire instead of accepting his poverty. He knew that, even though he was without a sponsor or support, he would someday come out in a big way. Flip went to the top of his profession and I used to watch his comedy program on TV every week. I felt like Flip. I could identify with the fact that I had to overcome negative attitudes in my own childhood.

I was the youngest of three children, an afterthought I guess, as my older sister was about to be married when I was born. As I mentioned, something happened to my Mom and mentally she checked out. I will never know why or how. But I never got to experience the love I craved from my mother. She was placed in an insane asylum when I was three years old and never came back. When Dad took me to visit her she did not recognize me and, in fact, the mental institution left me with deep psychic scars that I carry today. Dad lost all interest in everything, including me.

When I was little I thought maybe mental illness was "catching." Later, I believed this may be so because I got depressed a lot and my sister was prone to depression also. She believed she would one day wind up insane like our mother. As she outlived her insanity fears though, she became positive and "hurrahed" and praised the grandchildren until she passed away at 101! Long life is on my side of the family.

Instead of all this insanity drivel driving me to be negative, it helped me to study positive thinking and I became more and more positive. I guess there was some reverse "sly"cology at work here. Anyway, the negatives that were in my life made me want to seek out the positive and go the other way.

My only positive recollection in childhood was me telling myself that I was not going to be crazy and I was going to be a big man someday. I created self talk before it ever became a book or success course. But, it was not until I read *Think and Grow Rich*, and *The Power of Positive Thinking*, that I felt I had found the kindred spirit for which my soul hungered. I remember feeling relieved that I was not alone in defeating the demons of negativity.

Later, when I studied the Bible, I knew the name for the negative forces at work against me. If you want to remain positive, one thing you have to do is recognize the enemies (the world, the flesh and the Devil) and then defeat every one of these forces or thoughts that gets in your mind and life. It still is my constant job today to be positive, especially as aging is believed a curse in this nation focused on youth.

In my mind's eye, I see myself at my prime and go to those mental powers that made me strong and remain positive (if only in my mind). I am a rabid overcomer. I have to conjure up determination and persistence to find the positive in my life each day. That will never end until my last breath. I have to admit though, the hardest thing each day is to not live in the past. Make yourself live for today and your dreams of the future. It is better and it keeps you young.

As you can see, I did not come from grand beginnings. But look where I ended up!

XI

Never Give Up!

If I had to say one particular thing that makes for great success, it is that successful people never give up their dreams and goals. Discouragement is so easy that a big adjustment is necessary to clear out this subluxation above the atlas! Determined persistence means that you never give up, you never quit, you never completely lose heart and you keep going no matter what.

I mentioned the "thumb suckers" in my seminar. These are the doctors who usually feed on discouragement. I like to tell a story I heard long ago about a person who died and went to Hades. As he was being shown around, he saw that there were several doors to pass through. Written on one door was "Doubt," on the next were "Worry," "Hesitation," "Laziness," "Unbelief," and "Self-centeredness." Finally, there was the last door which was wide open. People were coming through it one after the other. So the person asked the Devil what this door was. "Well, through these doors pass everyone who is coming here, but the last door is always open because it is the most powerful force we use to get people in here." The fellow went over and pulled the door closed to see what was written on it. It read, "Discouragement."

When I would coach doctors who had failed in practice, it was ten times more difficult to get them going than other doctors who had not had an unsuccessful practice. All my clients wanted to grow, but the ones who moved along at a fast pace had never experienced failure. When I saw one of the doctors succeed who had come with failure baggage, I found that it was much sweeter for my heart to help them.

The failure syndrome, along with the discouragement that comes with it, leaves nearly unfixable scars. But once these doctors believed I had faith in them and believed they could make a step forward, they became successful. This was always difficult. As I said before, it is easy to be discouraged, not so easy to keep yourself moving forward after several steps back.

I learned early on that, even when flying blind, you have to keep going, if only for your spirit's sake. BJ used to say, "keep on keeping on." I guess he was the master of persistence since he had the entire world to convert to chiropractic and he took it on himself to create the philosophy and education for the profession. What a job he did! He was not perfect, and I have read and listened to many of his detractors, but I have yet to see as much work and effort put into chiropractic by anyone else.

Dr. Hershel Standford was a model of a persistent man. It was when I got out of college and started working for him that I learned I could use this trait for myself. I modeled him. Hershel was a very successful chiropractor in downtown Atlanta. When I quit my job in St. Louis, he hired me. I had learned a lot in St. Louis and could speak on the radio.

When Dr. Standford hired me, he tried to underpay me. This is when I first made up my famous axiom, "Those that ask get; those that don't ask, don't get." I taught this axiom to every chiropractor I ever coached. After Dr. Standford told me what he was going to pay me, I stared him down and reminded him that I had experience. I told him I would do a radio show for him too, but I wanted twice that salary and the room up over the office to live in. He agreed. Just like that.

From then on, I started to "ask" everyone for the rest of my life. I can't help it. I never take the first offer or the first price. Maybe if it is a super deal, but even when it is a "steal," something tells me that if it is so cheap, I could see what would happen if I offer even less, so I ask. I'm persistent to get my own deals, my own way. Sometimes people get mad, especially now that I am giving my money away, but I don't care. No one offers me free lunches and I don't want "meals on wheels" ever!

After working in Dr. Standford's office, I went out on my own. Dr. Standford practiced with a system called G-P-C (God, Patient, Chiropractor) or the Box on the Wall system. I did not like the system, so I started out with my brainy ideas and almost failed until I saw that I needed to place all my benefits and emphasis on my inner chiropractic conviction and my desire to help people.

Even today, I am asked for the magic bullet of practice success. There is no one thing, but rather a multitude of systems that make up a successful practice. Primarily, it is the ability of the doctor to clear out the subluxations and his passionate desire to help as many people as he can. This keeps the practice gaining momentum. You have to be the best doctor for each patient. You still have to connect the dots with determined persistence. But, when there is no passion, the "Mo in Momentum" soon equates to an average practice, or worse. This was especially true for me, because I started out in the all cash practice era. I still made sure my patients got much more than they paid for in my offices.

One day, my classmate Dr. Lorraine Golden, called me. She said she had started this children's center in Louisville, KY (Kentuckianna) and that the government had given her some old Army barracks for a clinic. She was persistent to get this clinic off the ground. I could feel her intensity through the phone. All she needed was money. So I started having these fund raising meetings in Albany to help her out. I tried to get Napoleon Hill (of *Think and Grow Rich* fame) to come speak, but secured Clement Stone instead. He was one of the richest men in the world and he respected chiropractic. He started Combined Life Insurance and was the first ever to write a policy that covered chiropractic. He was an inspirational speaker and we had every business person and chiropractor from all around come to these meetings. Lorraine said the money we raised from these meetings held Kentuckianna together for a long time in the early days.

I made millions in the twenty years I was in the consulting business by encouraging other doctors. At first, when I started out, I thought I could beat them over the head and berate them, hoping to get them so mad they would rise above my accusations. The opposite was true. They became even more discouraged. They would not pay me and, finally, just quit. So, I changed my tactics. No matter how lazy they were, or how much they sucked their thumbs, I would believe in them! I found some strong points to believe about them and I worked with this positive point until they finally became successful.

If you want some old sage's advice: never discourage anyone. Don't even have them work on their weakness. Find their positive points and get them to concentrate on using their strengths. We all need positive strokes. Let it be said of you that you never berated another doctor (not even a medic) and that you never gossiped or maligned anyone. See what blessings come your way when you have an encouraging spirit. And when you never give up!

XII

Let the Crabs Escape!

I like to tell the story of the crabs in the big tank you used to see sometimes in restaurants. I still see some lobster tanks, but not like the old days. Watching the crabs in those tanks got me to thinking about how people act. The crabs were always trying to escape from the tank, but as soon as one gets to the top, the crab underneath him would pull him back down in the tank, trying to craw up the side wall. So I invented the "crab lifestyle" doctrine in my consulting.

I started teaching my doctors and CAs about the crabs in life that pull us down when we are trying to get to the top. No one said it would be easy, trying to succeed and escape the negative forces of the world. You cannot be successful if you are a crab or if you hang around with crabs.

I know good doctors with great success potential whose spouses were crabs. What do you do with a crab spouse who always wants to divert your attention from your practice, or pull you away from your practice to wait on them? What do you do with a crab spouse who has to make all the decisions? Sometimes these decisions affect the doctor's business in a negative way. Most of these spouse crabs really thought they were helping out with all the crabbing and pulling the doctor in different directions. So how do you deal with a crab who thinks he or she is right and knows just what the doctor mate should do at all times? As a consultant, you forget about them and never bring it up. You can't change anyone. Just go right to the doctor's strengths and work on that.

I remember a female doctor whose mate tried to control her professional life as well as their home life by crabbing at her if she did not do things just his way. To start with, I knew I could never solve the home problems of my doctors, but I could motivate them to work on their Treasure Map. Seeing the spouse clip out new homes, vacations, etc., seemed to get the emphasis away from running the practice. If I was able to effect change anywhere in their personal life it was by teaching this self worth doctrine: **Take Charge!**

If you take charge of something that no one can move you off, you are in control at some point. This creates a power position that sets you up for success and causes the spouses to leave well enough alone. Make up your mind about what you really know you can do and do not let any crab get into that space, especially in practice. If a crab patient tells you what he or she is going to do, or what you need to do, you are in trouble. Take charge! Your knowledge of clinical chiropractic puts you way above your patients' understanding, but you have to bear in mind they may have doubts and problems that need solving, in addition to their clinical issue.

Your job is not so much to convince them that you know best as it is to explain why your care plan and procedures are for their benefit and that, if accepted and followed, will produce better results. You may have to compromise on your scheduling or other plans for them, but never compromise what it will take to give them the best care.

I used to have everyone in my classes stand up and holler out after I admonished them. I would say, "What do we have to do in our office with our patients?" And they would yell out, "Take charge"! If they were not screaming it out they had to keep doing it over and over again until they sounded like they wanted to take action. They probably wanted to take action against me for making them feel goofy. But I wanted to make a point. You have to escape the crabs. You do this by taking charge of your life — your practice, your staff, and your patients — and making the decisions you have to make.

Spouse problems are hard to overcome; pessimistic friends are next. You can't be successful and gain momentum in practice if you have doctor friends who are crabs. These are the people who want to tell you five reasons why you should not be doing something. They want to tell you the economy or the weather or something will cause your practice to slow down. These people usually mean well, but they can hinder your progress, dampen your enthusiasm, and/or minimize your glory. Don't drop their friendship, just take a vacation from them or change your relationship.

One thing I did was to have my new doctors bring their doctor friends with them to the next seminar. Sometimes, I had my doctors get new friends. Usually with each class that came through our program I had each person send their office newsletter to three other doctors in their class. Many made new friends who were on the same quest for success they were and could relate to my changes and success strategies. With your old friends, give them love and concern, but you may not want to take them into your business/practice activities.

When your practice starts gaining momentum, they may want to get your advice and that you can share. Keep your hopes and dreams mostly to yourself, or within the confines of those who are on a similar course. This inspires you to go forward. I remembering telling my new doctors not to visit other DCs in the town they picked out. If there is a really successful doctor who is so busy you can't get in to see him or her, then try to visit this doctor and pick his or her brain about the area. Usually, the very successful doctor sees no competition and will welcome you to the area. When you are ready for the open house start up, then visit all the other chiropractors in town and invite them to your open house. By then, you are so busy getting ready to blast off any negative they give you will not be taken to heart.

General Dwight Eisenhower said, "Let's never waste a minute thinking about people that we don't like." He was talking about crabs giving off negative energy. When you spend time daydreaming, slandering or maligning someone, this negative energy hurts you the most. Not only do these bad vibes hurt your spirit, they hold you back from receiving blessings. Now I'm talking about apples and oranges. The positive thought processes when making plans, dreams, goals and working hard are completely opposite from negative thinking and speaking.

You have to really watch what you say and think. That is why you watch the company you keep. That is why you just find edifying friends and people who boost your spirit and make you feel you can go forward, instead of concentrating on the negatives of the moment. As I said, we all have enough negative baggage to detonate. Take care to destroy your own negative thoughts without having a friend who is always looking at the pessimistic side of everything. What helped me the most when I was growing my practice was to find doctors to hang with who wanted to move ahead and were doing about what I was doing. Then we could have friendly competition by seeing who could get to the next level first. That is why I recommend a coach for everyone who is serious about increasing his or her practice. A wise coach can help you grow, celebrate your success with you and show you how to get out of debt.

Robert Kennedy's words echo in my ears, "Most people see things as they are, and say why? I dream things that never were and say why not?"

Remember, I mentioned to you earlier that I found a positive point in all of my doctors on which to build our relationship? This positive point started me thinking about good things that could happen for this doctor. Big dreams are never enough for success. They are only the beginning. Dream as big as you can, but remember you have to create action steps and not let the crabs influence you.

Inside every one of us is a genius. In our own ways, you and I are both geniuses, but in our own way we are goof-offs too. The klutz in us may be stronger than the genius, but that is where this thought must stop. We have to see that we must develop and use our genius side. I like to see my friends laugh at me when I told them, "I am a genius; if I only had a following!"

It is not unusual to count all your talents on one hand,

but it is very unusual when a person develops even one of these talents to its maximum. Any good athletic coach can tell you that, "You can't put in what God left out." You have to concentrate on your talent and be devoted to its development. If you can't run fast, it does you no good to go out for the track team. So get the meaning here. We are all given talents and skills but we have to be committed to developing them. I recall that line in the movie *Chariots of Fire*. The great sprinter, Eric Liddell, was talking to his sister in the movie. She kept giving him her crab advice to stop running and go on with his future in missionary work. What he said stuck with me. It went something like this, "*I believe that God made me for a purpose, but He also made me fast. When I run, I feel His pleasure.*"

This is how you want to feel about your success. You can take your practice to the highest level you want to go if you are willing to pay the price and you develop your skills. Strive for more capacity and persevere. One thing you want to do with the crabs in your life is to make them stop preying on your weaknesses. One of our Practice Consultants' rules was to:

"Dwell on your strengths in public,
Work on your weaknesses in private,
Keep both to yourself."

Like I said, we have few real gifts. When you discover the gift, start using all your time and energy to develop and use that talent. God gave Tom Morgan a music talent. He said he could just hear a song on the radio and sit down and play and sing that song. He had bands all the way through high school and college, but he felt called to chiropractic. He said that when he got to graduation, he sold his electronic piano and stage clothes and turned down an offer to travel with his band. After he burned these bridges, he was fully ready to be a chiropractor.

People who display great talents have merely gone over and over this talent until they are effortless in its delivery. My success as a doctor came from watching other doctors and learning from the training they gave me as well as being persistent with my patients. I knew what they needed and I encouraged them to follow through. That is the way a great doctor becomes even greater.

When I would talk to doctors who wanted to quit chiropractic and go into something else, I had two thoughts for them to consider. First, did they really want to throw away all the time, money and effort it took to become a licensed chiropractor and get into practice? Next, was my belief that 99 percent of all the doctors I coached were destined to be chiropractors. They had to persist in their practice and believe they could overcome themselves. It was not some fluke that they decided to become DCs. They had latent doctoring talents that they did not know they had and all of them had some innate drive to serve people.

I watched doctors in clinical settings and wondered how they had any patient referrals. They always surprised me, as some became the most successful of all our clients. Even with marginal talents, if you couple your talents with positive coaching and business initiatives, you can have major success. The doctors who wanted to quit or move locations believed the grass was always greener somewhere else. This is not always true. You take your sorry self with you when you quit and go elsewhere. Most of these doctors who I convinced to stay put in their location made it big. It was above their atlas, not the town, etc. where the problem was.

So doctors, if you are reading this and feel like chiropractic is maybe not for you, think again. Without even knowing it, you were led into this profession. My advice is to forget your negative excuses for being a chiropractor and change thought patterns and start saying to yourself that you are supposed to be a chiropractor and you are going to give it all you have. Believe that chiropractic is for you and then get to work!

I will always say that chiropractic is the best kept health secret on the planet. I see what it does for me and for others and I will have faith in this thought picture more than what anyone else says positively or negatively.

One thing I had problems with in coaching was to not run out of patience with those doctors who got the Boot Award for poor performance in practice. I just knew they could do so much better. My prayer was to motivate and stimulate them to move forward. Like I said, I ran into a key for me when working with the last in the class. I stopped focusing on what made me negative about them and looked only at their strengths. At the end of the day, only God can deliver you from your faults and weaknesses, but when you turn into the wind on your strengths and work hard to maximize your talents, you can be as successful as you want to be. Remember I said this!

One of the early success books that had great influence on me convinced me that 90 percent of the population lacks self confidence, so I did not feel so bad being in the same tub with the other timid/lazy/whining people. I was not afraid to work long and hard, but even with this, something was lacking. What I figured out I had to do was get out of the tub of poor self esteem and build some sturdy walls of self confidence. I was already a doctor. I knew what to do to help sick people. I could do my job, but I had to find a way to communicate my work better and motivate my patients to refer. Success became a process of acting and becoming a great doctor, reaching the next level I wanted to reach.

When you get the crabs down to a minimum, the next habit that will hold you back is to hold the belief that you have to doubt everything and everybody. Sometimes you feel you have to examine everything so much and so long that you lose the power to make positive decisions and move forward. You become an information gatherer. You just like the process of getting information, but not the responsibility of making a decision or of working toward one central goal. I found that doctors like this were usually filled with some latent guilt. There was some negative they believed about themselves that held them back. They could dream. They could write down goals. They could gather up all our consulting material (more information) and they would do the work, but they could not make instant decisions and live with the consequences. These were the doctors who I had to teach how to take charge of patients. They had to focus on what they wanted to look like and be like to patients. They had to pick mentors who could help them. To these doctors I told my favorite story about the snake and the mountain climber.

One day, when a mountain climber ascended to an unusually high level, he saw a poisonous snake coiled up among the stones. As he instinctively prepared to kill the snake, it cried out to him, "Please put me inside your warm jacket and take me back down to a lower level where I can be warmer and more comfortable." Feeling sorry for the snake, the mountain climber placed the snake inside his jacket and took it down to a lower level of the mountain where the air was not so cold and damp. When he reached inside his jacket to remove the snake, it bit him. In dismay, the mountain climber asked the snake why it had bitten him after he had done so much to help it. And as he lay there dying, he heard the snake reply, "You knew what I was when you picked me up."

With doubt comes fear. With trust comes confidence. You have to wear out your fears, pray them away and work at detonating them constantly until you like your positive manner better than all that pessimism. You have to find that decisions provide the next level you want. We all know what fear does to us, so why do we pick this snake up? I guess there is comfort in our old negative thought patterns. So we let it creep in at times of weakness. Oh, we can blame our family, friends, the government, teachers, everyone, even the dog, but it is still you who overcomes, and you who do not overcome.

If you get bitten by some untrustworthy snake, person or scheme, just leave it behind. Write off your losses, as we say in business, and move on to something positive. Learn by your mistake, but don't dwell on it until you are in a puddle. The less energy you give defeats, the less importance they will have in your life.

That is why it is so important to build positive patterns in life. Get up in the morning and exercise, then read the Bible and positive thinking books, plan your day and look forward to moving ahead in your service to your patients. Look for the miracles in your practice, get testimonials and celebrate healings. Replace a bad habit with a positive good habit each week.

Learn to celebrate the greatness in chiropractic and your practice. Where else can you duplicate your service hour after hour until it is everything you want it to be? What a place to return to each day! Our practices should be a refuge for us. When the snakes of life bite us in the butt, be thankful for it! We grow through suffering so learn to use life's little bites as reminders to not do that again and to replace this negative with a positive new goal. It is tough to move ahead and forgive yourself and others; the entire ministry of Jesus points to this project for us mortals. Work on it!

You have heard success is ninety-nine percent perspiration and one percent inspiration. There is something to consider here, as we coaches like to get into your head and believe that one percent motivates the other ninety-nine percent. But, in the end, it is you who has to try. It is you who has to climb up and slide back, over and over, until you turn the corner toward lasting achievement. Still, sometimes we don't learn our lessons in life. But believe me when I tell you, you must try, start, work and persist with determination. I can't say this enuf!

XIII

Alone at the Top

"Everyone wants you to do well, but not too well, and especially not better than them!"

And remember, "No one can make you feel inferior without your permission."

I say this to help you encourage yourself. Remember, there are two voices talking inside your head. One is not good and responds to the negative, worldly events and forces around you. When you hear this voice (the one that says you are not worth anything and that your ideas, work and goals are unreachable) change the channel! You want to tune into your wee small voice. Now, I don't know if this is God, innate, the Holy Spirit or what, but there is this voice of an encourager inside you and it will feed you positive actions, impressions and ideas.

You also have to look for those friends who will encourage you. In fact, you want to associate with only those who can encourage you. An encourager like this is not an easy person to find. I am such a person. I know about victory and defeat. I know how to deal with rejection, fear and loss of worth. I am overcoming them even though I am close to 90 years old and I will overcome them until my last breath. As I said, I made a living by encouraging chiropractors who I felt did not have the positive strokes at home or in the profession. I believed in them and they knew this to the point that they believed it and started making changes toward success.

"Family and friends are hidden treasures.
Seek them and out and enjoy their riches."

When you are really growing your practice, you have to know it will actually come down to motivating new patients. They have to come on a regular basis, sign up for care plans and follow through. Then, they become your practice family for life. Doctors tell me about the new patient who rejected them. I always ask if they can see these rejections as stepping stones to success to not dwell on them. The Holy Bible teaches that you only grow from defeats and hardships.

I knew how to help the doctors rise above rejection. They had to believe that their report of findings and recommendations were the best for the patient and believe the patient trusts them because their concern and love was above all doubt and rejection. I have my doctors tape their new patient interviews. I advise them to keep listening to the tapes they make of those patients who accepted care and followed through. Now, if you just slop through the Report (ROF) with that rejection patient, maybe you deserve what you get? But the key is to always do your very best at the ROF and do not accept rejection. It was probably not personal. You will never have all the answers from your patients.

I have seen new patients go out and borrow the money to start care when they did not have it. Some were not even capable of paying it back because of their condition, but they had faith that they would once again work and that chiropractic care is important. Why would they place such a value in my care? I believe it is because I accept only compliance in my mind. See only the good you can do for people you serve and live in the good they are getting being under your care. Believe in yourself and your systems. That's the unwritten mental code of being a full faith chiropractor. You live what you have seen to be real in your practice. This includes the results you can't always explain scientifically, but that happened and others can have the same fantastic results. Still, you have to encourage them.

I read where 25 percent of everyone we meet will reject us and our ideas, regardless of personality or circumstances. When I read this, my mind turned it this way so it read better in my mind: after rejection comes compliance.

If they don't take my program this time, they will come back and get it later, or go to another DC along the way and take his or her program and stick with it. That is why I always liked some "cold" patients. Referral patients were ready to begin care, but marketed patients who came in with the coupon or gift certificate did not have this made up mind to begin care. Sometimes, they were mostly focused on the idea of getting a deal on the first visit. These were the patients who would challenge me. I got to the point that I prayed for these patients and thanked God for the opportunity to make a chiropractic impact in their lives, even if it was not time for them to become a complete patient. Everyone likes referred patients. They are already clued in on my procedures and plans. But these "cold" patients were the great challenge. They were a chance to give out a lot more than they paid for. When I did the exam and told them my findings, they were impressed to the point of completing care. Here are my three points of contact:

1) Could they trust me with their health?
2) Did I really care about them?
3) Did I know what I was talking about?

The stats reveal only 50 percent of these marketed patients were serious about care and received the results they were seeking. So, what am I saying about rejection? It's all in your attitude and how you deal with it and how much you really like patients who are shopping for a deal. I tried to overwhelm them with chiropractic.

I like to think the best Harris success law is to "Keep on Trying." Never give up. That is why I put determination ahead of persistence as my favorite rule. I keep saying this because this was what I kept saying to myself. I had to learn that evaluating everything will only get you blue and depressed. You can think too much. There is a time to live in where you want to be, not where you are. Just like you don't have to understand the laws of success, just use them. They work, so learn the plan and work the plan. Continuing to try is the real secret.

I don't understand aerodynamics but I buy plane tickets and fly everywhere. You have to step out in faith. You don't have to understand everything. I can't tell you how many times I told doctors to just Do It! I started these "Do It" days and tried to get this idea to sink into that part of the doctor that needed encouragement. No matter how hard it seems, you have to keep trying. Success was a new idea to these people. Maybe it is to you? Let's use Dr. Seuss's philosophy:

> "You have brains in your head;
> You have feet in your shoes.
> You can steer yourself,
> Any direction you choose."

Chiropractic natural health care is still a new idea. That great motivator, Tony Robbins, says that any new idea goes through a three-step process before finally being accepted:

> First, it is refused and ridiculed.
> Next, it is viciously attacked.

Lastly, after it has been thoroughly analyzed and evaluated and it keeps working and growing, it is finally accepted as a self-evident truth.

The idea is often acclaimed as a major breakthrough or discovery while the previously persecuted originator of the idea goes unrecognized.

Certainly chiropractic has gone through these three tests. Why do so many people still have doubts and rejection? The answer lies in their ignorance and the anti-chiropractic propaganda still out there from the medical/drug world. Plus, the reason I like best, is because everyone has been trained in the wrong way. The training that everyone has is medical. First, go to medics, expect a diagnosis and a blast of drugs, and then hope you never have to go back until the next crisis.

Chiropractic works in the opposite way. We require time and repetition for the adjustments to help innate change our patients for the better. It takes time to get sick and time to get well. We want to get them excited about our results, but more importantly, we want to get them educated in our systems. We want them to have our healing and health philosophy and we want to build faith and understanding in long-term care — making that chiropractic gene vibrate in their souls.

My next law is to Make it Happen. Instead of just letting things happen **to** you, make things happen **for** you. Stop living in the victim mentality. Take charge! I'm getting revved up again! You have to know the real value of your services. You never lie, cheat, or steal. You always give the patient far more than they pay for and you always strike a fair deal for cash patients. Open your eyes and see your great value and chiropractic's great value. See things as they really are, then go over this mantra all the time as part of your self talk. Look for patients who want what you have to offer.

I used to get upset when I had a really conceited patient who was intent on bossing me and the staff around to fit his or her own agenda. I soon learned not to take it personally. Instead, I learned to ask a lot of questions they could not answer. I learned to put them off for more tests later. I kept my take charge attitude to mean that I should withhold my great service to them until they found some respect for me and/or chiropractic. So I made demands they had to meet in care. I even got strong enough to tell them they could come back when they were ready to follow **my** agenda. They could only come back when they were ready for me to be the doctor. Even then some did not get it.

I trained my doctors to Watch Yourself. Too often, you may be looking for a hidden agenda, a negative, or a reason to fail with a patient. This is pessimism at its finest. The devil can put a rope around your neck and pull tight on this type of mental attitude. This chapter is about presenting yourself as the answer to the new patient's problem. Take those bonds and shackles off your attitude and move forward in confidence and belief.

I remember dealing with a regret I had. For a long time in my life I failed to save and invest. Then, when I found that I was good at it, investing and saving became my outlet or hobby. I also found that, no matter what your income is today, some of your earnings can be put in savings. But, you must have your mind right and the system for saving in place. Saving is like giving your money away. You have to be trained to do it because basic human nature is to spend it on yourself (selfishness) and hold your money tightly (greed). The opposite will set you free. Savings will give you great options in life. Giving your money away will bring great blessings! It always works if you work it first. It is like that with all success. Just get behind the laws and put them to work. Don't question them or look at minor set backs. Keep trying! Here are some more of "Harris's laws."

❑ Stop procrastinating.
❑ Establish deadlines.
❑ Turn your wishes into goals.
❑ Take control of your own destiny.
❑ Create your own future.
❑ Understand yourself in order to better understand others.
❑ Visualize what you want to accomplish.
❑ Practice the mirror technique (more on this later).
❑ Make a Treasure Map and a list of goals.
❑ Keep telling yourself what you want your practice to be like and that you want this more than anything in your working hours.
❑ Increase your efforts with each increment of success.
❑ You must know that God created you to be a great chiropractor to help His people.
❑ You are unique and nothing can replace you at this moment in time.
❑ Never take your eye off of the bulls-eye (goal)!

I kept the following remark with me, I can't remember where I picked it up, but it is one I think of often:

"When I see a fence across my path
I'll make a gate, or I'll climb over
But I'm GOING ON!!"

Steven A. Lavelle, an internationally known educator said there are three components that must be in place to accomplish your goals.

1. Desire
2. Suspension of disbelief
3. Dedication

If any of these are out of kilter, you have to shore it up. You have to Do It!! Got that? DO IT.........NOW!

XIV

Tell Them Again, Sam

"You don't get what you WANT out of life, you get what you EXPECT." —Nido Qubein—

When dealing with patients, you have to expect the best, but you cannot get the best unless you are a good communicator. One of our best training seminars dealt with communications with patients. This is the reality. You must establish a chiropractic relationship with the patient that makes communications work. I broke down my intent when speaking to patients into three parts.

1. Use all your education, skill, study, background and beliefs when you tell the patient something new.
The way you present chiropractic is always new to the patient. Never assume patients can understand what you are saying unless they first get tuned into your thought patterns. You remember the old doctor's cliché? Patients know how you feel about them before they understand what you can do for them.

I wouldn't put my entire belief system on this line, but it is worth your consideration. You must give off the scent of healing. That is why you want to tell the patient what you are doing as you do it. This keeps you on track and the patients will either get into this chiropractic groove or they just daydream. Certain words and concepts develop interest in what you have for the patients and get the patients to move away from their symptom focus. We want to have patients move to the point of relating their problems to the cause (chiropractic subluxations). When they become interested at this point, we have communicated one fact to ourselves — we have taken charge.

Have you ever had patients who could not stop thinking and talking about symptoms, visit after visit? I used to think that something was wrong with me. I took the history. I talked about the condition and what was causing the symptoms but still the patient's entire focus was that one thing — feelings/symptoms. The focus never shifted to the goal of the doctor. I used to think that it was because the patient had gone to so many medics and been brainwashed into gushing out symptom after symptom until someone listened. But that was not true. After I practiced for awhile, I learned how to break this communication barrier with this type of patient. I would kindly ask the patient to do me a favor, saying,

"Now Jane, I know you have that pain in your neck. I have located it and told you what is causing the problem. Are there any questions as to what I told you that is causing the pain and what the adjustment is doing?" If the answer was no, then I asked the patient to follow me in my special procedure each visit. Could she wait until my chiropractic exam and adjustment were finished before telling me how she was doing today?

This usually broke that negative medical/symptom barrier and gave me a lot more chance to go to the next point in the patient's chiropractic education. When I would walk into the adjusting room, I would look at this patient and see if he or she was ready to blurt out the symptoms. If I sensed this would be the case, I would speak directly to the point.

"Mary, I want to examine your cervical spine before I tell you how much improvement you have made today."

2. Explanation of Care.

If I did not explain every area, he or she would not understand the next step. I used a lot of different stories and ideas and word pictures in my explanations. Simply telling facts does not mean patients understand. Have you heard the one about the man sitting on a park bench? There was a dog playing around the bench and a stranger who liked animals stopped and asked the man if his dog would bite. "No," said the man on the bench, "my dog does not bite" When the stranger bent over to pet the dog it bit his hand. "Hey, I thought you said your dog doesn't bite?" The man on the bench said, "My dog does not bite. That's not my dog." Even though he told the stranger that his dog did not bite, he failed to tell him that this little dog was not his dog. Give your patients the full explanation and ask for feedback along the way to see if the understanding is there.

3. Repetition.

If you do not repeat the salient points, patients will not remember. What they remember is what counts. When they get home and spouses ask what the doctor said, they should come out with the primary points of knowledge. Attention spans and retention spans can increase with visual aids, charts, take-home pictures and information. When you give these out, underline the exact problem and write in the margins. It is here that you have to use proper words that conjure up images that stick in their minds and that bear remembering.

Patients are mostly thinking about themselves. This is even more true at your office. I like this verse from the book *God's Psychiatry.*

"I gave a little party, this afternoon at three
T'was very small, three guests in all,
Just I, Myself and me.
While I drank up the tea
And it was I, who ate the pie,
And passed the cake to me."

Patients want their needs met. That is all. They are not there to make friends. When you earn their trust as a doctor, then you have a friend for life. I remember as a young doctor I once had my tie crooked all morning. When I glanced in the mirror at noon, I wondered why no one said anything.

The truth is, they did not see my tie. They had their mind on themselves too much to bother about me. This is when I knew that all I had to do was to get their mind set on what I was doing, the adjustment, and their point of progress. Then, they would start listening to me.

If I talked about the weather or current events, they seemed entertained but not educated. Don't make this mistake and spend valuable office time visiting with them (that will come much later). Teach, don't visit. When I talked about the weather, they would leave no more motivated or empowered than if they were at the barber shop. I wanted them to leave my office with chiropractic knowledge and excitement about their adjustment and results. This was my intent and I worked hard on this point. Plus, I knew if they could learn to talk about chiropractic, they could get other people excited about coming in to see me. I always expected all of their family and friends to someday be my patients. It happened that way with my intent to communicate and teach chiropractic principles. It can happen for you.

XV

Bust a Gut

When young doctors and students ask me about opening a practice, they always want to know what I think about joining clubs and becoming involved in the community. The first rule is that you have to be recognized as the chiropractor whenever you are outside your office. I advise young doctors never to get into organizations as just a regular person. You want to represent chiropractic in your group, town and area.

You have to "bust a gut." That means you do everything possible to draw attention to your service as a great doctor with results everyone wants. When I moved to Albany, Georgia, we joined the First Baptist Church. There were six or seven hundred people there every Sunday. I was head usher, then Sunday School teacher and then Sunday School Superintendent. I wanted to do these jobs, plus it helped me get to know people as the chiropractor in town.

You see, you have to hold your power close to your chest. You have to create a mystique about yourself. That is why testimonials are still the best advertisement. People see these results and it creates a mystery in their minds about how someone, like themselves, can get well with this so-called chiropractic adjustment. I did not join all the service clubs. You have just so much spare time for the community outside your office, so I picked the church. Of course, I was always my preacher's chiropractor. I took care of the staff and just about everyone in the church at one time or another. I liked spiritual things. It all appealed to me. Do not go into clubs or other organizations in town without really having some genuine interest to serve.

You want everyone in the club to know you are the chiropractor so I did not join until my reputation was established. That way, I was adjusting these fellow members at the events and eventually all of them and their families were patients. Whenever I stepped out of my home, I was on stage. The stage I set for myself was as a chiropractor. I saw myself as being a great one with a powerful adjustment plus a powerful message and great results. I wore my reputation on my sleeve. This is because I made sure everyone knew me and knew what I was about.

Being focused as the chiropractor in town brought me much attention. After I worked so long and hard, I sold my practice and then I blended in as just a person in my area. People still sought me out with their ailments and I referred them to my old clinic, but I was not the healer I used to be before I retired. After this quick bout of retirement, I had to go back into practice. I found that I had to heal the folks! First, though, I had to get that fire in my belly because I wanted to go full steam ahead again in practice and consulting.

Today, I tell doctors to join these business groups where you meet for breakfast and every person in the club gets to talk about his or her business. When it is your turn, you get to speak three minutes on chiropractic and give some testimonials about a certain condition. The thing to do is get someone to raise his or her hand with the condition you are speaking about and give them a special visit that day. Meet them at your office that day. Then, the next time it is your turn to speak you can have this same person get up and tell about their chiropractic experience in your office. Their testimonial has more power and influence than all your efforts to toot your own horn. The key, when you are young in practice, is to intensify your efforts and demeanor. You want to "bust a gut" trying to get your healing influence out in the community. It is not easy to draw attention to yourself and your service but never stop trying.

I still like radio because, as I mentioned, I always had my own program and a column in the local paper. My voice, combined with my words, made me an authority in town. People would stop and ask me if I was Dr. Harris. Now I liked being famous, but this was a self contained town so it was easy to get into this position. When I moved from the fifth floor of the bank building to my new clinic on Main Street, I had a special room built to broadcast my radio show. It was there that I interviewed patients and they testified about how chiropractic helped them after medicine had failed. The medics in town did not like me much. But there was never anything bad they could say about a cured case.

In those days, we did all we could to get people to try our new healing science. Dr. John Stokes had great programs and we used to send each other tapes. I used to revise all his programs to fit myself. It is like we do sharing ads and marketing today.

When I think on the power of the radio, I always think of that special patient, Minnie Sue. Before I built my new office, she called me one day and said she believed every word of my broadcast and that she wanted to be a patient of mine but she was impaired and had a hard time driving, parking and walking up any stairs. I told her I would see to it that she got in my office. So I worked it out with her that she would come at noon and honk her horn twice. When I heard the two honks, I went down on the street and helped her out of the car and parked the car for her. Then I came back and carried her in my arms up the stairs. She walked slowly on the flat, so she did pretty well once we got upstairs. It is one of my fondest memories. She told everyone about how much we cared for her. In those days, I would do anything to help a patient, especially one who already thought I was the greatest doctor in the county.

These broadcasts had more effect than I knew. I did not take them lightly and made sure I got myself prepared in mind and spirit for these programs. There was no pre-taping. Everything was live and I wanted be in the right frame of mind. The way I used my mind then and today was to have this firm belief factor set deep and solid in my psyche. I pictured patients needing chiropractic care and praying for something, some doctor or event, something besides a life of more and more pills. I was going to give them a better idea. When I believed something so strongly, I worked with my higher self to make absolutely sure I was convinced chiropractic is what everyone needed. Then, I would be able to convince my listeners that it would be right for them. That was one reason my programs were so successful. Plus, when you work at making your beliefs and results true in life, even though anecdotal, no person can make you negative. That is the way I am with chiropractic all the way! That is the way you have to be.

Don't ever let other people, or your lower self, beat you down. I can't tell you how many nurse-DCs I had come to my seminars who could not get that nursing persona out of their system and take charge as the doctor! Plus, changing the spouses whose medical friends (make more chiropractic friends today) left them nagging their husbands or wives about the fact that they needed more money, acceptance and whatever. I had to cram chiropractic into them with all I had. Unless they believed as we do and wanted to live the chiropractic lifestyle, they would always feel inferior. And that means they would listen inside to their lower voice whispering the vibrations of rejection, jealousy and materialism. It won't work any other way in a chiropractic home because everything medical you do makes your doctor/spouse negative.

I found that in large cities you have to approach new patients in a different style. You have to get next to people personally. You can't just run an ad in the paper and they come running in to see the great doctor. You have to touch people's lives. I advise doctors in larger cities to do screenings or give talks and just find ways to put their hands on people. I remember my good friend, Dr. Gene Sparlin, in Atlanta. He used to go to his patients' houses and give coffee talks. Then, he would examine them and make appointments for each person to come to his office. He built his practice that way in its early days.

Sometimes your efforts, or your spouse, or the environment, are not the reasons you hold yourself back from success. I have found that, more than anything, it is attitude. Like I mentioned above, if you really believe in what you are doing and that everyone needs chiropractic, then your daily mission is to get everyone else to see your position in chiropractic. You do this by teaching each patient about chiropractic every visit. So, are you doing that? Then what is holding you back? The answer is your motivation. Momentum in practice is based on keeping the wheels greased. Once things are rolling, you can't go on vacation for two weeks and expect the momentum to be where it was. You can only do this with a long-term maintenance practice. Even then, you have to stay focused enough to keep the practice at an even level.

So what do you do if you are not burning with the desire to convert the world? What do you do if you are not willing in your heart to "bust a gut" trying to get to the next patient or taking your practice to the next level? You have to find a coach, a mentor, or someone you can emulate. You need a doctor who has been there and done that. This is a person you feel you want to be like or strive to please in your efforts.

I have seen a lot of spouses pull down their doctor-mate because the mate does not believe in chiropractic with all his or her heart. They take drugs or go to medics and in general show a lack of faith in our principles and practice. When this happens, a dark, gray veil starts to cover the chiropractic soul of the doctor. If you don't live for your family's needs to be met first, then you do not understand how vital it is to have a home team who wants to live the chiropractic lifestyle and show themselves and the world that you don't have to live with drugs and medics in your life. They need to understand that chiropractic is based on wellness principles and that you are disciplining yourself and your family to keep subluxation free, have regular exercise, take organic nourishment, and keep spiritually and mentally in tune.

When you do this, you are in the chiropractic lifestyle. This is the best style to live in my book! My mind goes back to that tiny lunch café next to Palmer. The "Hillside Lunch," (we called it the Hill-slide). When I was in school, my friends and I would sit there for hours and make the "Hillslide Pact." It was about pledging to live our lives without the medics or drugs and believing that innate could do more for us than any person or doctor. I know it is not always possible to remain that rigid, but I still live in this ideal state of health for myself and everyone. I am still passing on this chiropractic vision to everyone who will listen. It is what I know as truth.

XVI

Chiropractic Greats

BJ Palmer was the most influential person in my young chiropractic life. He was almost unapproachable at school so we hung on every word at his lectures. He spoke to our class often, but clinic was the hour we never missed. The class was in the auditorium and BJ would call students and patients up on stage and "nerve trace" their spines. Then, he would "read" them with the Neurocalometer (NCM) and tell the patient just what to expect from his special adjustment. He spoke of his adjustment having that "something special." We all wanted that! He taught us how to talk with all the power and authority of a true healer. This was something all of us yearned to duplicate with every subluxation we found.

Of course, there was only one real subluxation at the upper cervical level, but BJ could nerve trace the entire spine relating everything he found to the atlas, axis and where the spinal cord pressure existed. There are, of course, 450-plus trillion nerve fibers at the foramen magnum, spinal cord level, but only BJ knew where the pressure was for each patient. I still believe he did! We young students were in awe of him in almost every word and action. He was more than an icon. He was chiropractic itself.

I saw him in his prime of life. It excited all of us to see him perform. His books were legendary and we wore the covers off of them, reading them day and night. All we wanted to do was to sit in the cafeteria, drink coffee and talk about innate, universal, BJ, Mable, DD, and the mission ahead of us as chiropractors. BJ's wife, Mabel, taught public speaking and anatomy. She was a gifted teacher and she went to a medical school in Chicago where she studied to be a great anatomist. Rumor had it that she spent too much time in the x-ray labs with those old machines and that too much radiation put her in an early grave. BJ was lost when Mabel died.

Their son, Dave Palmer, was in my class. He was the playboy of Davenport. Of course, he had access to the Palmer millions, so he always had new cars, clothes and the only job anyone knew of that he had were the chores BJ gave him — feeding the alligators that were kept in the basement of the mansion in the winter. BJ was a hard taskmaster and did not take to Dave's speakeasy and Flapper-filled lifestyle. BJ went to bed at nine p.m. every evening and was an early riser. He wrote his books all day, lectured, studied and traveled to defend chiropractors all over the country.

Dave went to the Wharton School of the University of Pennsylvania and took over many of the family's financial ventures. It was said Mabel and Dave voted against BJ in the Palmer corporation, leaving BJ out of all financial affairs in his later years. There's no stopping history though as Dave became sole heir and controller of the Palmer estate in 1961. I mentioned earlier that I had gotten Dave and BJ together at BJ's summer home in Florida just before BJ died. This last meeting helped patch up a fallen relationship and later Dave would thank me for it.

I got to speak to BJ from afar, like most students. He kept mostly to himself. It was said there were only a few really close faculty and friends in his inner circle. BJ would be the one to fire anyone from their jobs at the Palmer enterprises so he never got too close to them. I started going back to Lyceum every year and made a name for myself as a very successful chiropractor. It was at these Lyceums that I got to be in BJ's presence and speak with the great man. As I mentioned before, I got BJ to come to Albany, Georgia to dedicate my new clinic. When he got off his personal plane, I made sure there was a great crowd of chiropractic doctors there with their families and patients. BJ addressed everyone and gave great speeches as only he could do. It was a great event. Later, he dedicated one of his green books to me. It would be the highest honor I would receive in those early years.

I used to love Lyceum when the field doctors came back to school. They were so positive and we students picked up their vibrations and dedication. During Lyceum every Palmer grad who could beg, borrow or save enough cash would return to Davenport. It was the time to get rejuvenated, learn the latest technique, meet other chiropractors, old friends and students, and to hear the great BJ. He always had something new he was working on.

Every Lyceum BJ would put up banners, flags and his half-block long Barnum and Bailey style circus tent on campus. It was a famous Quad City symbol, announcing to the world that thousands of chiropractors would once again descend on the River City. I came into school in the thirties and watched in 1935 when BJ brought out the NCM and Hole in One (HHHIO) Toggle Recoil Technique. BJ found a better way of giving the Toggle Recoil adjustment on a solid (then Thompson drop) side posture headpiece. BJ and Doss Evans invented the first thermography, the NCM, and the "Tempograph" to read the spine in a consistent position.

The "Chirometer" was another instrument he sold, a single thermocoupled probe that he put next to the mastoid process to measure bilateral temperature at the atlas. Dierfield leg checks, stereo x-rays and then the famous drop side posture Toggle Table, invented by Clay Thompson, filled the flagship at Palmer. All of us had to have every invention BJ could come up with and it made him millions. It also made the HIO days into the most powerful and exciting in chiropractic history. I never lost my love for upper cervical work. I came to appreciate the atlas, axis adjustment more and more. I feel that it is the key to spinal balance. Later, I studied under John Grostic and used his upper cervical technique, along with full spine adjusting, during all my years in practice.

Not many years ago, I followed Guy Riekeman when he

became president of Palmer and even donated the research building in mine and Jo's names. I was proud that windy day I stood on Brady Hill and looked out across the campus, but the powers that be at Palmer did not appreciate Guy like I thought they would. When the opportunity for Guy to come south to Life University presented itself, I was the first one to speak up on his behalf to the Board. Boy, am I glad I did this. It was my last great decision, plus, may I dare say, a decision that will change the course of chiropractic history. Guy has brought Life University back to the largest campus and largest chiropractic college in the world.

I was not allowed on the Life campus or to take part in early Life College days, but things change and I feel I have come home again as I dreamed about this great college in the south land and here it is, bright and shining. I recommend everyone reading this today get behind Life. You will see the world change from Atlanta. It changed once from Davenport, but it is Atlanta now —mark my words!

HIO Technique (Hole In One)

As I mentioned, I love Dr. Roy Sweat. He adjusts my atlas these days and I guess he has researched the upper cervical spine more than anyone out there. I understand that, to be proficient in his AO technique, you must do all the spinal anatomy dissection over again with him in the lab. The only problem I saw with upper cervical HIO only was that we had to face patients everyday who had low back pain and only give them an atlas recoil adjustment on the neck.

In those days, we read their cervical spines with the NCM until we were blue in the face, trying to get a pattern to reveal a consistency that indicated the need for the atlas to be adjusted. If the legs were level, the NCM out of adjustment pattern, and palpation normal, the patient was declared clear. That meant, no matter how much the patient was hurting, no adjustment was given on that visit. The patient in pain was told it was due to "retracing." It took a better man than I am to do all this and tell patients to leave in pain because they were clear. This is a hands-on profession and I felt something had to be done each visit. I had to adjust the low back when the patient was in pain.

Now, don't get me wrong, about two out of ten low back pain patients would be free of pain after the atlas adjustment, but the other eight always concerned me. Because BJ was so insistent that he had found the cause of all dis-ease with the atlas/axis subluxation, I wanted to honor him and his research, but today the lumbar/pelvis are adjusted right along with the atlas. There were loads of full spine technique classes off campus, but we were threatened with expulsion if we were found at a clandestine seminar. Everyone took these courses anyway, just in case we needed to know how to adjust the other 22 vertebrae. The lumbar-pelvic technique was mostly lumbar rolls and P-A thrusts on the lumbar spine. One of my classmates was Clarence Gonstead. He was a mechanical engineer before he came to chiropractic. It would be Gonstead and Thompson who took the full spine technique to new levels of proficiency. May God bless these fine doctors.

BJ was the first to use Thermography. Some said he was too unbalanced on the financial profit side. The rap on BJ in the HIO days was that he was making millions leasing the NCM and the Neurocalograph (NCGH) which graphed the spinal reading on paper. The NCM was a hand-held, encased instrument. The "GH" indicated a graph. The goal was the same as today: to get to the point of clinical proficiency where we need not adjust if the patient's subluxation was stable and there was no nerve interference. Trying not to adjust and over adjusting has always been the community flaw in chiropractic.

While BJ was getting more dogmatic on his technique, other schools and full spine techniques were being developed across the country. This only got BJ more and more upset and arrogant about HIO. He called everyone who adjusted below the axis a "ChiroPracToid" or "Medipractor." If you used modalities with the adjustment, you were a "mixer." BJ and the HIO doctors were "straights," thus the profession became locked into an extraprofessional battle that still smolders between the political camps of today.

We called the HIO days the technique era in chiropractic.

Before BJ got the profession hopelessly locked in technique and philosophy battles, there was unity. Early on, DD Palmer and BJ worked together and taught every doctor a "mobilizing" type of full spine adjusting. Every vertebra and its adjacent joints were adjusted to mobilize the patient. They had the right idea with all the motion, but our technique needed to get more specific adjusting. The emphasis was not on the technique in these early years, but rather on the amount of good you could do for the most patients.

Chiropractors in those early days were trying to stay out of jail, develop the science, get state licensed and beat the medics in the art of healing. We did just that. In fact, we got so powerful that entire state legislatures would license us despite the efforts of the elite, wealthy medical lobbies. This happened because of cured chiropractic patients in high places pressuring state senators and representatives until they had to license us. It is still amazing how a new health profession could get licensed in 50 states without organized medicine ever once showing any interest in what we were doing to help sick people.

After we became licensed and gained more recognition, BJ was getting old and his dogma was fading away. It was at that time chiropractic began the political and educational eras in the profession. As I said, after BJ died, Dave took over. He wanted unity for all chiropractors. He brought in many techniques at Palmer and he wanted more education and prestige for the profession. He also wanted real scientific research. There was no government money for research going to chiropractic so we had to suffer there for many decades. But Dave did influence the national associations, our state boards and state associations to increase the DC degree to six years instead of four.

I remember many in my class thought there would be no more students with such high entrance standards but the opposite became true. In fact, the colleges got bigger and bigger. Now it is typically eight years (four years of undergraduate studies and four of chiropractic) and I think that will not make a hoot of difference in our growth and development. In fact, today the research money is kicking in and we are on the threshold of such power, authority and under-standing concerning the subluxation complex that I look for the six o'clock news to one day headline the great efficiency chiropractors have over all other professions in healing. Just you wait.

After I became successful, every time I would go back to Lyceum there was a leadership role for me. I started teaching and lecturing on practice building. It was nothing formal in those days, but from this need I first saw in our doctors, I knew I was just the person to inspire, motivate and train doctors about how to be successful. I could teach a success formula that really worked. You just had to believe what I taught, then take the action step and work it. Those with mighty ambition and drive got more out of it than most. Look at your chiropractic spirit today doctors. How much do you love chiropractic? How much do you appreciate the opportunity to teach patients about innate and chiropractic? How much do you want to be faithful to your profession and to give something back to it? Become a great doctor and a great giver, not a taker.

XVII

Innate does the Healing

"Of what I call God, and fools call nature."
—Robert Browning—

It is Hippocrates, the father of medicine, who is credited with separating the human body into two parts. First, he spoke of the physical, which he relegated to doctors, and then the spiritual, or the soul, which he turned over to religion. The two would not be mixed. This left medicine as a mechanistic science in which doctors had to find the chemical or do the surgical procedure to make the patient well.

No prayer could be used and nothing but empirical explanations would suffice as their science. God was not mentioned, nor the fact that within each of us is the bios or life force. This could not be included in the doctoring professions. Chiropractic was the first to call itself a natural profession, utilizing the natural recuperative powers of the body for healing the patient. Thus, we developed our philosophy of health and staked our claim to natural methods and procedures to treat the body. Only chiropractors helped patients realize they had to take part in the healing process and could learn health habits that helped this life force inside of them change them for the better over time. It was chiropractors who created this innate or inborn philosophy. Medicine created a sickness profession, waiting until the patient was sick and educating them to put full faith in doctors and chemicals to change them back to normal.

Let's take a look at what happens when we are sick. We see people moving along in their lives, doing what they want, or following their careers until one day they become sick and are flat on their backs. Then, all of their self-seeking action and positive mental energy change. Essentially, their worldly routine stops at that time. Everything is different when your physical body does not or cannot do what you want it to do.

Can your doctor, any doctor, speak of God while treating you, helping you return to the normalcy you seek? Do the mechanics of treating this condition with this drug or even with an adjustment have a place to put God in the assessment? What about all the human mechanisms we rely on — self sufficiency, positive mental attitude, creativity, self motivation and perspective? They usually have to wait.

I can still hear my patients groaning at me while unable to rise to a standing position. They would tell me they didn't have time for this back pain. Remember the last time you had a fever? Remember a time when you were disconnected from what you wanted to do? Do you remember how weak and unaccomplished you felt and how you had to lay in bed and sleep because the body only healed itself when you were asleep? Do you remember waking up in the morning, anticipating what healing progress you made in the night? It did not matter if you had obligations to meet or if you were rich or poor, young or old. It mattered that this "thing," this virus was ruining your waking moments, disrupting what your schedule was *supposed* to be.

Did you blame God for creating viruses and germs? Did you take any credit or blame for running your resistance/immune system down below its adaptable limits? Was your life timed at that sick period to interface with God, the Devil or faith? Did you put this faith in a person who went to school to earn a degree called "doctor"? Did you put your faith in a blind pill made in a factory, or the bone movement of an adjustment? Was your anticipation for healing determined by a human solution from a human person, a doctor?

Chances are good that you looked for human solutions and thought of your illness as a human problem, not a spiritual one. So where does a sick person place faith and prayer into the healing process? Can you get well if you are an atheist? I've seen both get well time and time again in my office. When you look at that line where spiritual and religion cross over into medical or chiropractic care, where is your doctor in all of this? Since we are not taught along religious lines in school, doctors usually are at a loss for explanations how or even why to incorporate spiritual thinking into the treatment plan or outcome assessments.

As chiropractors, we neither give drugs nor perform surgery. When we adjust our patients, the nervous system in the spine triggers the body's innate healing mechanisms and the human organism starts changing for the better. Evolution, when defined as simply "change over time," is one of our healing principles. The human body is always changing. We adjust patients to change them for the better. The adjustment makes the body evolve to a positive position physically. Still, we have difficulty speaking of God to our patients or about the life force God breathed into each living person.

We also have problems relating what this innate intelligence is and how it helps change us back to health. Like all doctors, we are taught not to mention God in our report of findings. In fact, there is no teaching in this area. It is as if we are taught not to mention the spiritual side of human life when all of us know that healing (health) is about mind, body and spirit. As doctors, we must consider only science, and with science, we must have a world view of what affects our patients. I think I can prove to you that all science is bent toward negating and not mentioning Intelligent Design in any of its postulates or programs. This is too close to religion and that is not to be mentioned in the world view today. Scientists can lose tenure and jobs if they mention God in their work.

We have been conditioned very strongly over the past decade to be politically correct. This is the secular world view. It was conceived to put an end to prejudice and discrimination. I think it has helped a lot in this regard and this is good. But this slant in our thinking has conditioned us and taken us to places far removed from prejudice and discrimination.

Public officials are afraid to comment on any deviation they used to think of as wrong or that they had been taught were morally or ethically against their family doctrines or own personal moral opinions. They are afraid to mention any position dealing with morality and deviant behavior that could be construed to be aimed toward a specific group or profiling our fellow human beings. Not counting most crimes like murder and robbery, we are to believe that if human nature can think it up it must be fine and accepted by everyone else regardless of the moral or ethical situation.

Remember our scenario above, about how sickness takes you away from worldly activities? This world view wants us to think you must accept it as human nature to believe you can control your world and that all progress is made through human viewpoint and human intervention. No one can say, "God controls history." It is this human nature viewpoint that believes government can legislate morality or create agencies who can house, support, rehab, train and create a useful person to society. There is truth here, but mostly this falls into the line of believing human solutions can fix the world's problems.

Have you heard of the bills introduced in Congress in the past few years that deal with Hate Crimes? This is a human solution used in reverse. While accepting the world view of introspection, forbidding any prejudice or discrimination, the authors of this bill bent this ideal toward their own personal desires (to eliminate all religious programming in the media). They want to make it a crime if you mention in public, for instance, that you must pray to Allah three times a day, or you are not a complete person without Mohammad or that, unless you are saved by faith in Jesus Christ, you will go to hell.

If someone complains you are affecting their life in an adverse way with religious statements, you can be convicted as a felon and sent to prison. This bill looks harmless on the surface until you see it could wipe out the first amendment and stop freedom of speech and religion. There is no doubt this bill is aimed at destroying religious freedom in this country. There would never be another religious program broadcast over the media. Plus, it could be used against doctors who are trying to talk to patients about where God fits into their health disciplines and/or the healing equation. Doctors could not talk about a creator who breathed life into us or who placed their innate intelligence inside every human being and what part this intelligence plays in this healing process. This alone could land the doctor in jail. This bill is another attempt of putting this new world view in place to control and restrict a segment of our society.

Medical Eugenics is said to be the worst blight on historic medicine. It involved that period in medical history when doctors sterilized thousands of our handicapped citizens. This event can attest to the abuse of power doctors held over these patients where the decisions of a few affected the freedom and rights of others. Evil Nazis in WW II took Eugenics to another level of human exploitation when doctors experimented against the will of the individual. But this is another instance of this same type of world view taken past its limits. These doctors' views were much like dog breeders, when they personally mandated the necessity to destroy a dog that would pass on obvious physical handicaps, thus helping the breed.

Thank goodness Eugenics was abandoned. However, even today there are medical people who want to control population segments and advise putting birth control drugs in the water supply of third world countries. This is another example of how a few believed they knew how, why and what was best to decrease the world's population explosion. It is no less conflicted than the fact that state laws are being passed today that would make it mandatory for certain synthetic drugs to be injected into every child. They would give the state permission to take your child against your will and inject them. This type of world view seemed good to some people (and profitable to the drug industry) but it can take away our freedom.

This ranks right alongside of those law makers who believed they should pass a national alcohol prohibition law (1920–1933) and that this human solution would end the consumption of alcohol in this country. As you can see, there is a kernel of good that can come about from restricting freedoms, but history has shown that restricting freedom in any way will destroy a society. Even if we don't like what is going on around us, still we must have individual freedom to help ourselves or destroy ourselves. However, it is that very freedom that made our country the greatest in the world.

I agree that a world view is very important. But the world view I want to support is one of central unity. Germans call it "weltanschauung" or the Big Picture. It involves the sense of the whole picture of the universe, begun and controlled by a sovereign God. This cosmic framework gives vitality and meaning to all we do. The Christian writer Dr. Larry Crabb said it better, "The real issues are not theological issues where life is brought down to an irreducible minimum, the issue always is God — what we make of Him and how He fits in our lives." King Solomon, my Masonic patron, says (ECC. 6:10), "Man is not able to contend with God, nor are we stronger than He." It is useless to be in conflict with Him. C. S. Lewis put it well in *The Problem with Pain*, "To argue with God is to argue with the very power that makes it possible to argue at all." I don't have the answers how or where God should be taught to doctors and where this fits in caring for the sick, but I know HE MUST BE IN THERE.

Unlike medical schools, chiropractic colleges teach vitalism. I will write all I've learned about this great principle in chiropractic. This may be our GREAT principle, as it keeps us a natural healing profession, separate from drugs and surgery. Chiropractors must teach the recognition and dependence on the body's innate intelligence, i.e. the recuperative powers of the human body that bring about healing. This is in accord with all natural healers. There is a condition like a pinched nerve that can cause severe pain. All I know and witness is, after the adjustment, the innate intelligence of the patient starts to change the evolvement of the organism back to a normal state (health).

Health then, is not an absence of disease or symptoms, but rather a homeostatic effect, stemming from its neurological and physiological balance. The adjustment changes the patient's structural stability and this will bring about health when coupled with proper diet, rest, exercise and stress control (can we say here, a balanced spiritual life?). As vitalists, we study the body in disease and in health. Instead of figuring out how to change the body's chemistry from abnormal to so-called normal, we learn what nerves control the organ or part and how to diagnose the subluxation that could adversely affect this. We are pointed toward the five factors mentioned above to help the patient return to a normal position (health) without any drugs or their negative side effects. We teach patients that this is the part they play in getting well in our office. We must tell our patients,"The power that made the body heals the body." This to me is spiritual, but not religious.

Does organized religion have a part in the doctors' healing message to our patients? All of the major religions of the world have sects and services involving healing. They tend to be inclusive entities without drugs or adjustments. In place of this is faith and prayer. When approaching a doctor about faith and prayer in their healing work, most doctors will be respectful, but unable to comment. Some will even pray with the patient for God's healing after their procedure. This is as it should be but it is not within the context of the media's world view or with medical/scientific academia.

Can I talk to my patients about God? There is no law against it as I write this. But, it may be a freedom that could be in jeopardy. No profession knows better about this freedom than chiropractic. Our struggle for state and national licensing laws and Medicare inclusion will attest to our great country's freedom. Let us continue to guard it well.

XVIII

Encouragement: the Elixir of the Soul

We are here to lift other people up. When we do too much for ourselves, we soon become miserable. Self focus leads us to mind, body and soul degeneration because it does not agree with spiritual law. That is why I taught my doctors that losing yourself in your intent to help other people does something for you that nothing else can.

You must get in position to lose your "self." For example, when you are busy in your office, soon you seem to be on auto pilot, working unselfishly, doing what needs to be done in a smooth, effortless, soul-fulfilling way. I always tried, in my consultant work, to give doctors a "baker's dozen" so they would receive more than they paid for. That alone sometimes made them follow through with my programs and become successful. I always tried to coach the spouses of the doctors too. I wanted to teach them how to be positive for their spouse who was struggling to grow the practice. Also, I wanted to help keep them from spending all the profits. I wanted the spouses to get the saving concept since they are the support system for the doctor.

Without a support system, you will fail. Even if you have all the finances you need, your spirit will wane without the love of family, friends and your support system. You have to make memories and share your memories. You have to be responsible to someone each day. My time without my wife Jo stunted my life. I have asked other women to marry me, but it just did not work out. If I could rewind my life, I would have looked harder for another wife and burrowed in deep with her family and friends. A woman can teach a man a lot. I am sure of this, but now the autumn of my life is on me and I am alone most of the time. Oh, I get up and go to the office. I have a driver who I feel is my friend and I also have Jane at the office. She has become my eyes and ears. But when I go home, it's just me. Your family and friends are very important, so don't shut them out.

How long can you practice?

I have old friends who still go into their office and adjust patients. They are very fortunate doctors. Even though I retired and started consulting, I think back at what a privilege it was to care for patients. Chiropractic is so great, so helpful, and you can use a technique you learned forty years ago that still gets sick people well. What an amazing profession with which to be involved!

Let's look at the peak production (saving) years you have and how long the old body will last leaning over that table. This is what I found to be true: I know a doctor has thirty to thirty-five years of practice productivity. This is the time when he or she can really save. Time can run out for you though. My advice is to begin to save on the very first day in practice. As I mentioned, I advise everyone to put ten percent in savings from the very start. It is easy to lose that ten percent; putting it somewhere, and not touching it, that's tough. Mark my words: you will be more proud of this savings effort than anything you do in practice.

Have you ever heard any DC say they saved too much in practice? If you talk to any older doctor, ask if he or she could have saved more. Ask older doctors if they could have given back to their college and profession more than they did. You will hear the same things over and over. You young doctors have the chance to start from the beginning by giving, instead of taking. Save! You must be free from being in debt to banks!

I remember my days of being a spender and high roller. I had to have an airplane to fly around to my clinics and seminars. I thought I was big stuff. I never lost sight of my weaknesses though. I was too tight with a dollar to keep pouring money into that airplane. I like to say that I never got bigger than my britches. By that I mean showing off or trying to impress others with material things took second place for me. Oh, I wanted the glitter of material wealth when I first started having money. My ego wanted to show the world my success so I bought things to show off. I burned up my share of dollars, but I got hold of myself and started saving and living slightly below my means.

Jo was never pretentious in any way. I could always count on her to stretch a dollar. I always tried to make every dollar spent count for something. The best I could do was help people so I tried to concentrate on this and my family instead of on what the Wall Street advertisers were selling on TV. I found out that if I "had to have it" my emotions were talking and that was not good. I started developing a rule for large purchases. One was to give it a week and then go back and see if that car or whatever meant so much to me. Next, was to shop three of the same item to make sure I was getting a good deal.

I am glad I never reached the point of being satisfied with my achievements. At my pinnacle, BJ recognized me to the entire profession at school and in my home state of Georgia. He dedicated the book *Fame and Fortune* to me! I was puffed up then! It was one of BJ's green books. It was sort of like being asked to join the board of a Fortune 500 company today. Yes, I was touched when BJ told me he was going to dedicate this book to me. I started to cry (something no one saw from me, ever). I got to know BJ by going back to Lyceum, donating to Palmer and getting BJ to come to Georgia on occasion to speak and promote his instruments and chiropractic.

One time I took my two chiropractic nephews, Bert and John Boutwell, to Florida to see BJ. I wanted to discuss the formation of FACE (Foundation for the Advancement of Chiropractic Education), my nonprofit charity corporation, with him. I sent BJ a telegram saying we would meet him at this restaurant on the Sarasota pier at 12:19. BJ always prided himself on his schedule and time discipline, so I was testing him. When I got to our hotel, I called his home and the housekeeper said he had other plans for lunch and that we could come around at 5:00 to see him. That is about really how important I was to BJ. He was a good host.

When we got to his home and started discussing FACE, he was very helpful and encouraging. Then he said for me to get up out of my chair and follow him. We went to his private room where he had his big typewriter with the roll paper in the top. He showed me where he was writing a new book, *Fame and Fortune*. He then showed me where he was dedicating this book to me. The tears started flowing. I could not help it. I was trying to stop those darn sniffles, but they were tears of joy and BJ was smiling. I think BJ innately knew that I had planned to give back to the profession and that I had prayed about this since I was young.

When I started making big money, I felt that it was the thing to do with the income that would not be needed personally by me and my family. As I mentioned before, I had promised God, that if He would make me a success, I would do all I could to help others with the profits. That day, in that little room, when I saw that BJ really recognized me as someone besides another hanger-on or someone who wanted something from him, it touched my soul. BJ dedicated only one other book to a chiropractor. This chiropractor was Lyle Sherman, for whom Sherman College is named.

My wife Jo used to tell everyone that I was always busy doing three jobs at once. She would also tell people that no one she ever knew could get more done in the amount of time there was to do it in than I did. I took it as a supreme compliment and worked even harder. Jo was proud of me and my success. She was my mainstay. When she bragged on me, my reason for going on the next day was fulfilled. She got more out of me because of her encouragement and saying nice things about me to my family and others than any person before or since.

I won't say our marriage was perfect. In fact, it was far from it! I did stop hollering at her and I can't remember her staying mad at me very long. Jo was smart. She still did what she wanted. Jo was raised with a strong father figure in the home. Because of the domination of her father, I watched my step. One time, when I was setting goals, I wrote that I would start on a course to encourage Jo. I had to work hard to develop the habit.

When I saw the results of encouragement in consulting, I tried it out on Jo and the kids. A lot of it was not accepted with the kids because I missed so many chances when they were younger. However, Jo really warmed to me like never before when I took it on myself to look for her positive traits and brag on them. I believe with all my heart that she was the greatest blessing in my life. You never move anyone forward by condemnation, brow beating, cajoling, dominating, nagging, or by force. God and that person ultimately have to move along by themselves. This takes a self belief brought about by encouragement and faith instilled by God and others to give you the courage and tenacity to make good things happen. Probably what it does most is make you believe in yourself and the great gifts God gave you.

It was this way with my clients. I threw out all their flaws, wiping their past slate clean in my mind. Then, I started giving them a new image of themselves. Later, I would ask the spouse to join me in this effort and when they looked for good things to compliment their doctor/spouse about, their marriage and practice took on new meaning. Remember how sad I was about divorces? Well, when this new habit of positive strokes became my greatest coaching tool, I also saw marriages become successful where before there had been strife and confusion.

When I started the Boot Award at our meetings, it was to bring up the lowest achiever on stage and make a deal with everyone in the room. I wanted everyone to write to this person, send their newsletters and newspaper ads, and in every way help this person to move out from the bottom. I taught each class how to encourage as a group. They would take the lowest producer and make a team effort to help him or her achieve.

I came upon this corporate effort of encouraging because of losing the non producer. I heard the small voice. Usually, these "boot" doctors were ready to drop out anyway. I really felt that I had somehow failed them and this was my last ditch effort. They just needed more encouragement than I could give. So, put your team at home and in your group to work. Remember what I am telling you here. Sometimes these "boot" award winners clawed their way up to success. When this happened, all the encouraging and work will be rewarded more than they can ever know. I learned this by really getting down inside my patients and caring for them more than any doctor they had ever been to before.

Just like I did with my patients, I wanted these doctors to know I really cared for them and no matter how defeated and rejected and unsuccessful they felt, I held great hope for them. They knew I cared. My intent was for their benefit and I really believe that even the most inept doctor has healing and benefit to give patients. Small as their vision was, I could see the light from their stars. I guess I had seen such despair and anguish growing up that nothing surprised me. In fact, no amount of negativity that these doctors threw at me was surprising or insurmountable. Yes, I held the hope for them, until they could hold it and feel it for themselves. Then I turned to the next person to care for, support and train for success.

Even now, I find young people whom I am holding hope for and, in some way, I will help increase their happiness, along with their success. So, look to encourage those around you. That is why, I believe, God still has me around on this earth. I think I have a lot of good years left to hold the hope for those who need it, not for those who want something from me, but for those who need encouragement.

A few years ago, I met with the billionaire Warren Buffet after he spoke at a benefit in Dalton, Georgia. I never heard such a humble man. It was that unspoken word of a great business person with a powerful desire to make a difference in this world with his wealth that struck me the most. I have owned stock in his companies for decades and this stock is one of my best producers I have to date. It is no secret why

Warren is so successful. He uses the formula that you can't out give the giver, or out snow the Snowman. Plus, he had real humility. Everyone could feel it, even from the stage. Buffet teaches that there is no way you can out serve the person who is dedicated to serve and you can't out last your billions. I was inspired to do more, to give more, and to look for the next person to put my hope and courage into.

This world has great wealth, but it must always be secondary to what you do for others. Don't offer any excuses for past mistakes. Rather, learn by them and try to do better today. Also, never stop trying to move ahead in relationships and in business.

XIX

Be a Leader, not a Follower

You can never move forward by whining and complaining. Complaining is easy, but motivating yourself and getting the job done, whether you feel like it or not, takes discipline and perseverance. You must motivate yourself before you can lead your patients to any point of care.

Most doctors react to what the insurance companies are doing to them instead of leading their team to overcome any negatives from billing and co-payments. Yes, it may be true that insurance is trying its best to discourage the patient and the doctor by changing the rules and coding all the time. But, if you complain about a part of your billing or management, then your entire team starts to whine.

You have to keep your team on the path of more service and appreciation toward patients. Just like the doctor has to see the patient getting better, you have to see the subluxations corrected and innate healing the patient. You have to know this is what that patient needs most right now while he is in front of you. You must always be in the leadership role with patients and staff. You have to duplicate your love, concern and maturity on each visit. You must act like you are 100 percent effective with each adjustment. You lead by example.

Your team members need constant training, reinforcement, support and motivation to put chiropractic into others. They only get excited if you help them get excited and tell them what you expect from them in the office. Just letting the CAs do their own thing until they "get it," will bring frustration, plus you set yourself up to be let down by that person because you did not lead them to the goals you had in mind for them. Never think your practice will glide along by itself. You must be the pilot and be aware of your team and project your vision of more service and more chiropractic to your community.

When I started to expect great things from myself, my entire life changed for the better. I think I went too far sometimes as I started to expect greater things than I really believed I could accomplish. I kept my nose to the grindstone and never let on that most of the time I was surprised at the great things that happened to me in life. That is where I got the persistence part of my plan down pat. I give myself pep talks so I will not sell myself short. I do not want to lose. Sometimes things don't come through like I expected or hoped for, but I use that point to learn something new in life.

You see, we all must learn from the mistakes we make. I catalogue them so that I will not make them again if possible. I always want to win. I did not always have a winner's attitude; I had to develop it. What got me through my mistakes and poor attitude is this principle: if I lose, I never accept it, but if I understand it, I can learn from it and move forward in hope. You have to have this positive attitude about yourself. It lets you pick up and move forward in difficult times. If you want to expand your usefulness and don't want to let your family, profession, or yourself down, learn to lead yourself first, then others. Lead patients to the chiropractic way of life and health. This always means a better quality of health and life for them.

I keep thinking of my goals. I think you should do the same. Keep that short list on your desk to accomplish today and this week and keep the long-term goals for New Years renewal. Yes, I like goals. I set them for myself and when I reach them I celebrate with a reward for myself. They strengthen me and give me inward power and peace. Sometimes I beat myself and then it is more difficult for me. But, usually, I set the goal and then forget the goal and go about working on my attitude and eliminating the lazy part of me I don't like.

When I start to invest in a new stock or company, I want to know if they are trying to be the best company they can be. I want to know about their track record and I want it to show more than just increased revenue. I want to know someone in that company who makes decisions and see if they reflect that winning attitude I look for in people and companies. I want to associate with people who win, as well as people who carve out a place for themselves in their company. I like people who believe they can do it and then go about proving their worth.

Salesmanship is fine, but I never accept the talk until I see the walk. I am the hardest person to squeeze a dollar out of. I know that about myself, but I like it that way. It frustrates those who want something from me. When I come through though, I come through big. Live to create big action. Look for your life and practice to expand and explode into mega profits and progress.

I already told you I made a deal with God. Later, I found it is Biblical to make vows and carry them out. But these vows must agree with God's law and God's word and they must make the world a better place. So, keep making spiritual deals. Keep pushing yourself to be better than you ever expected you could be. Learn to be really thankful when you excel. That means God is using you to make things better than they are.

My problem with aging is to not accept or believe that the time will come when I am not useful, when my desires will level off and stop. If you feel you are winding down in life, it is because you are thinking of yourself, not what God can do to use you to help others. My advice for you retired or tired doctors is to start training yourself (and writing this in your goal journal) to look ahead and plan ahead. When you rake the yard, cut the grass, or go to the granddaughter's band concert, do it with all the love and concern you can muster.

It was my intent to show my clients strength by my gifts and faith. You show strength with a good attitude and a small job/event done well. Remember I wrote about donating to chiropractic colleges that were struggling? Some of these schools I pulled out of the red and helped them become solvent. Because of me, things improved. I had to get to the key people and help them really believe in their mission as leaders in their colleges and the profession. Everything took on new meaning after that happened. I focused on the students, the new doctors who would be graduating from these colleges, serving thousands of patients because I gave a gift that held the glue together. I never know just what will happen with my gifts, but usually I am impressed with how far reaching anything I can give bears fruit for the future. Usually it is multiplied. I know it is supposed to be a law, but I am still amazed. BJ always talked about "how far reaching" things we think, say and do today can affect the lives of millions tomorrow. He was one of the first "quantum physicists" of his time. So join me today. Let's set our sites to do something that affects the world today.

Write your goals down in a journal! When writing your goals I will give you some suggestions. First, set lifetime goals once a year. A good time to do this is around New Year's each year. You will be surprised how fast those new years roll around. With these goals you brainstorm your mind for everything possible you could be involved in or might desire. As you know, I am a big fan of keeping the human spirit, our educated mind, in an optimistic, positive position, but I do know there is a missing link between reality and rational thinking as related to dreams, prayers and desires. Still, I believe in the supernatural and put as much stock in my prayers and dreams as I do rational thinking, maybe more! Have you heard the old saying, "What you can conceive and believe you can achieve?" Well, I don't hold complete stock to this adage, but there is some truth to it. So don't be shy. Write down everything you can think of that interests you. The following categories will help you get your thoughts in order. I list them in order of importance.

1) Spiritual Goals

In this list write down every contact point with God and every idea or desire you have to know and understand Him. Include your involvement with church, Bible study and prayer, as well as outside service. I like the Bible verse that says, "If you draw near to God, He will draw near to you." James 4:8

2) Physical Goals

Write down your ideal weight, that you want to be sub-luxation free, organically nourished, get adequate exercise, and have proper stress control mechanisms (spiritual mechanisms). All these things will help innate change you for the better and help your body stay 100 percent in normal function (health).

3) Family Goals

List every person in your family and write your goals for each of them. Then go to extended family and anyone who is on your mind. If you want your children to be chiropractors, start writing it down.

4) Practice Goals

How much do you want to make next year? Write down the equipment you want, remodeling, new clinics, multiple clinics, coaches, seminars you want to attend, etc. Now is the time to expand your mind.

5) Hobbies and Material Goals

Write down your involvement and goals in any hobbies you have or want to pursue. Material goals should be really big. Anything made by human beings is available to you and can be on this list (homes, cars, travel, etc.). I hope saving money is on this list; it is not glorious, but it is right.

All of these goals can be as detailed or general as you

prefer. Now, here is a consideration. I read where the Japanese studied goal setting and found written goals were achieved one third faster than those not written. When the goals were drawn out in pictures, the expediency increased to two thirds faster! So, if you want new equipment next year in your office, cut out pictures of the tables, etc. you want and paste them on a poster board (your Treasure Map!). Put this poster in your dark room or staff room and get the team to talk and think about these pictures. You will be impressed with the results.

Next year, at the New Year's holiday, take out the list and circle the goals that have come about. When the goals are in progress, write down their progress and re-list them along with next year's goals. Carry all the goals that are still true over to the next year's list. Of course, there will be some things you will not carry over, as they will seem ludicrous a year later. So drop those.

On your desk should be short-term goals or the "Do It" list. Like I mentioned before, these are things to do today, this week, this month. That list should be looked at daily and be out in plain view. The yearly list should be hidden away for your eyes only. Another good idea is to write down couples goals with your spouse. Use the same five categories above and make this list together. It is better to have a partner in crime.

The Pioneer Spirit

If you want to stop growing and expanding, just start thinking and acting like you can just keep cruising along doing what you are doing right now. Act like last year's plan will last forever and you won't have to work harder and smarter. Staying with the same plan might backfire on you because times change. I call the pioneer spirit that part of you that is never satisfied. It is that inner drive that is looking off into the horizon, yearning for fresh goals.

Are you seeing changes first, before they come to other doctor's practices? Pray for new ideas you can bring into fruition. If you are satisfied with your practice, it will start to slip. Remember, this complacency feeling is the start of burn out. Burn out is that time in practice when you want to quit or stop working and planning so hard. When momentum is swinging your way, ride the wave, work as hard as you can, save as much as you can and when that burn out time seeps in your life, you have saved and planned for it. You can sell out, or take off six months until you get that fire in your belly to serve somewhere else.

Listen to your inner voice. Look for opportunities to bring chiropractic to other areas in your community. Maybe you can bring leadership to your college or state and national associations. Go to the children's home, the battered person shelters, or a local sports team and expand your giving with your great healing knowledge and skill. Keep your pioneer spirit! It too is a sacred trust.

How important do you think you are in life?

Here is a concept I keep going over in my head. Never sell your deeds short. Never just think you are isolated in your office, adjusting patients all day while the world goes by. Get the spirit of our early chiropractic pioneers! Live for what chiropractic has to offer today and can give future generations. It's not important if we don't see all the progress that is in the future of our profession. Live for today and keep the faith for tomorrow.

Our early doctors toiled under threats of going to jail for practicing medicine without a license. Today, we have the greatest freedom and prestige our profession has ever had in history. Make the most of this freedom. Take special care to lead your patients to real health. Present your health class to new patients and schedule speeches to senior centers, church groups, businesses and service clubs every month. Keep spreading the word about how healing comes from within and that this profession is dedicated to health without more drugs and surgery. Present chiropractic as a better way to life and health. You will be motivated and rewarded much more than the people you serve.

While you are adjusting everyday, think of those thousands of DCs who leaned over their tables with less freedom but never flinched, never complained, and who felt positive that chiropractic was for the future and would someday be understood. The adjustments worked. These old chiropractors would not live to see all that has happened to their great profession. The fact that these doctors helped thousands of patients kept us in the marketplace and ensured our place, and that of the next generation of chiropractors, in history.

Our research will someday catch up to the clinical benefits we have all had the privilege to witness under our hands. We understand how it works, we just don't know all innate is doing after the adjustment. Someday we will understand more. That is exciting to me! It is always amazing how this chiropractic works. Those who think we should join in the medical referral system (as backache therapists) are not staying true to chiropractic. How much we protect our principles and practice is very important. I left that to our national leaders. But, we must be vigilant to keep it going in the right direction, patient by patient.

I really think the world will come to us and put us where we belong in the healing field. I saw state boards and state licenses come from the strength of the people, our patients, not the politicians. There is more strength in the average voter than in the king makers and politicians. We just have to keep doing what is right, making the right choices, leading the right way. We need to keep teaching and practicing a better way.

I see such dynamic leaders in our colleges today. These leaders, coupled with the talented leaders in our national and state groups, give me much encouragement. We must get behind these leaders and encourage them to stay the course. Then, we can fall in right behind them. Show your support for our leaders, just like you show yourself as a leader. I have chosen to put my bucks and trust in the future and I never plan to quit this venture. Long after I am gone, the Harris Trust board will work on my directions. I always want to give to the colleges and research. Never let the ideal profession and practice become any less than your most ardent dreams and desires. It will happen. I believe!

XX

What I Wanted to Change

Doctors ask me what was the most disappointing part of my consulting career. I do not hesitate to tell them. You might think it was the disappointment I felt when I could not help a doctor, or when I did help the doctor but they would forget to pay me or, worse yet, when they showed no respect and did not refer other doctors to our program. You see, I spent all day calling my doctors and getting names of their friends to call. I liked talking to doctors, encouraging them to come to our next class. I knew we were good and had a good program. I would get the referral doctor to call them and testify about our worth. We could make a difference in their practices.

But, no, the thing I wanted to change more than anything else with our doctors is the fact that there were too many divorces. This was my biggest disappointment. We had a lot of husband/wife teams come to our meetings. It takes a team to make a marriage work and grow a family and it takes a team to grow the practice to a successful level. I have seen a lot of doctors reach mega dollar practices and then get divorced.

I was hurt mostly by the pain and anguish suffered in their divorces. The children never understood and were always caught in the middle. That was really sad to me. The couples would show such disrespect, as if the person who helped them the most should be shoved aside. It got to me somewhere in my soul when this happened. I began to hate divorces and when I heard of them and I knew the people, I

would sometimes call and plead for them to get back together. I saw couples reconcile and, when they decided to
make it work again and show respect for God's way and the
sacredness of their covenant, most of the time their marriages were better than they ever had been. Of course, that
makes my theory correct: hard times make better people.
Life is about choices. Who your mate is and what you are
going to work on in your marriage are possibly two of the
greatest choices you will ever make.

Mid-life will get a doctor. Also, after ten or fifteen years,
the doctor, who can practice with his eyes closed gets bored.
He starts looking for some way to fulfill the need to stimulate the ego. He may buy a red sports car. He may desire to
live on the golf course. He sometimes starts finding other
things, and often other people, to stimulate him. That is
when a lot of these divorces start occurring.

You have to watch this world we live in. It has no respect
for marriage. It tells you it is okay to have multiple partners.
It tells you everything is alright, just do what you want, act
as you will. The idea of "you deserve it" will jump up and
bite you big time. So listen, the sirens of the world can destroy you. Below is my check list for keeping the marriage
together. Now, remember, I was not a perfect husband or father. Maybe there are none out there, but I believe now,
more than anytime in my life, that you have to work on your
marriage, not just let it go along. I was a flawed husband
and parent, but I did the best I could and that is what you
have to do.

If you can't negotiate your problems and you yell and
fight all the time, go to a marriage seminar or counselor.
When you're my age, you know you could do better if you
could do it all over again. That's a given. The first thing to
remember is not to take your spouse and family for granted.
Any indifference will come back and destroy your home and
marriage. Marriage is the most personal, most intimate,
most satisfying relationship you will have with another person on earth. It is also one we are the least trained for. So act
as if you do not know it all and as if you need continuing
education. Each year you need to do something special to-

gether, just the two of you. Make sure you are reading books on the relationship and have weekly guides and checks to keep you moving forward in the marriage. Here are some ideas.

Have a date night

Have a certain time every week when you and your spouse go out together. You can vary the place but not the time. Do not talk about office problems or the kids. Try to talk about yourselves. Talk about what you want to do on vacation, how you feel about each other, and what you can do for each other. Try to say something really intimate and focused about the spouse. Focus on the positives of your relationship. Hold hands, look deeply into each others eyes, and/or pray together. Think of the love you started and where it is today and tomorrow. Pray and give thanks for your marriage and family. To grow your marriage, let your love for each other come out on these dates. Just the time you spend on the date will spark a better life. Remember, women tend to like warm fuzzies, while men like the facts. If you are like me, we men need to work more on the fuzz.

Go on a marriage retreat

There are great retreats available for married couples. When you get in a group thinking and learning and sharing about the power of the marriage something great happens to you. Try it! Next, both of you read a book on marriage once a year and then share the parts that mean the most to you with your mate. Even in the best marriages, this will still charge you with a reminder of how much you appreciate and love your mate.

Go the extra mile

Every week, find something you can do for your spouse before they ask you to do it. Run the sweeper one night or take over the bathing or bedtime chores, make the bed once in awhile. Cook and serve a meal. This shows you were thinking of your spouse instead of being moved along by the routine of life.

Watch what you say

Words are very important to a relationship. I found my wife remembered the negative things I said the most! So watch what you say the most! Don't sit around the kitchen table and gossip about family members, friends and others with problems. Cynical talk and gossip about others will kill a marriage, or worse, create a stagnant and unfulfilled life. When you find faults with someone, you do not pat yourself on the back because you are so perfect, what you do is degrade the human race and hold back positive relationships you could have had. Make this a rule: say something good about the person who irritates you. Try it today.

Have separate lives without separation

Each person must express positive personal thoughts, talents and experiences outside of one another. You don't have to be the center of attention. Let the wife be free to pursue her talents and have her own friends. Women, let the husband plan his day. Encourage him to plan his time off for a change. Do not try to run his entire life. Avoid this danger. Just because it is possible to run your husband's life, don't do it. Rather, let him make decisions. Tell each other how you value one another's talents and service. Men, you should think like I do; that your wife is the best person, best wife and mother in the world. Women, tell your husband about his greatness in chiropractic. Keep faith with him and the adjustments and do not go to MDs or give your kids drugs. This is probably the most important thing to your husband/doctor, next to you and the family. Remember the rule that no one understands chiropractic like your doctor/spouse so you must show the most faith and confidence in him/her and chiropractic.

Never compromise your principles, compromise your activities

There can never be just one person who gets his or her own way in a marriage. Agree to disagree, first with each other, then with the children. The spouse comes before the children so be careful about taking sides. The spouse also comes before friends and activities. Each activity that is shared by the family is better if everyone can agree that they will have the right attitude and will participate fully. Go with your husband to activities that he enjoys. In return, he must go with you on your interests and activities. Lastly, try to not yell and raise your voice in anger. It only raises your blood pressure and hurts your relationship. If you have un-controllable anger and rage, go to a support group for help. It is no weakness to admit you need help.

To close this chapter, I want to tell you that everyone must be on guard to watch his or her hormones. Even though you are satisfied with your love life at home, there are always the sex sirens blowing in the world. Every book, TV program, commercial, and piece of music speaks to this. You were taught in ethics class that the fatal flaw in practice is to respond when a patient makes a pass at you. Always resist a sexual encounter with a patient. Sounds like class, but it will come and you should make your firm resolution **now**, as you read this, **never** to respond. Take the doors off your adjusting rooms or have a CA come in with that pa-tient next visit. I have seen talented doctors destroy their ca-reer, family and lives with the wrong sexual response.

So make firm resolutions to yourself that you will not tempt yourself by thinking infidelity thoughts. Say to your-self and your spouse that you are faithful and want to re-main faithful. You are happy and are willing to work on your happiness. The grass is not greener on the other side. If there is no physical abuse, then I think a marriage can work, if you can take working on it seriously enough. Attitudes of discontent and unhappiness always creep in a marriage. It's the dark choice inside your head that welcomes and em-braces these thoughts.

Discontent is not always the fault of the spouse. Some people are just not happy and have to learn how to disci-pline themselves in the happiness direction. Happiness, like grace, must be given to a willing person. A person who wants to find happiness, make happiness and share happi-ness comes by this attitude naturally. But if you have not learned how to do this, it has to be an attribute you develop. Become that happy person today. This means being happy where you live with your spouse and kids. It also means being happy with your friends and extended family, and with the gifts and performance of your spouse and children. Happy and thankful — what a great place to live!

XXI

Don't Let Your Tickler Die

My good friend Jack Donovan and I have been room-mates at Palmer Lyceum for many years. His wife always bakes cookies for me. Thank you Darlene! Those cookies are some of the best I have ever eaten. Jack is upbeat and posi-tive (that is why I stay with him), but many of my old friends and classmates are so negative. They just don't real-ize what their negative talk and vibrations are doing to them.

One thing I always say to my old classmates and friends when they start to wind down in practice is, "Don't let your tickler die." You see, I learned to believe and know that when one door closes in your life, there is a bigger and bet-ter one opening up IF you don't let your tickler die. All you have to do to die on your feet is start thinking about yourself and your needs.

Nothing gets to me more than to see an old buddy who, instead of extolling the positive life we have had in chiro-practic, starts telling me his symptoms and conditions (worse than medical patients!). They even want to drag me through their surgeries and tell me the drugs they are tak-ing. This starts to make me sick! I always thought the red badge of courage and honor in chiropractic is to get through life without any drugs and surgeries. Now, I am not a com-plete fanatic. I have some organs that are not functioning at 100 percent and I have to have a pill now and again, but I don't want anyone to know it, especially these old chiro-practors. We have to carry the chiropractic flag for the young doctors. We have to set the example. I think it is up to us to be the example of long-term chiropractic care. Thus, we are the result of what innate is creating everyday inside of us.

These old doctors should know better than to unload their medical baggage on me. Keep that to yourself boys and girls! I don't tell anyone my weaknesses, and when I have to see a medic or take a pill, I sneak around so no one will see me and my hope is that this visit is only for a crisis. I know all drugs are for temporary things and I owe my health to innate and chiropractic. Any medic I have ever gone to will tell you I am the worst patient they have ever had. That's the way I want it. That is because I am a rock solid chiropractic patient, not one of theirs. I keep talking to myself, putting them and their practice in a compartment. I realize that their specialty is crisis care and sometimes I get in a little crisis. This does not affect my dependence and belief that chiropractic is the only permanent health system. I am not proud of it when I have to take a pill, but it may be necessary for me at this stage of life. So I look in my fellow chiropractors' eyes and say, "Tell me boys, what greatness have you seen in chiropractic today?"

What I do like to talk about and think about is that last adjustment that turned the innate healing power on inside me and made me come up in life. Usually, I stay in adjustment, but there have been those times when I needed and received that right adjustment, at the right time, and had such results that it made me love chiropractic all over again. When I visit my chiropractors I want one of their best adjustments. There is a young DC around the corner where I live now. I'm his mentor these days, Dr. Carl Amodio. I like that impulse instrument adjustment that Chris Colloca invented. Dr. Carl can really tune me in with that thing. Thanks Dr. Carl.

My all-time atlas line-em-up man is Dr. Roy Sweat. When my "tickler" sinks low, I head for downtown Atlanta to get Roy to straighten my atlas up. No one in the world can do it like the AO man himself. Also, when I see my friend Tom Morgan, I get his adjustment. I tell him I can get a "110 volt" adjustment from any doctor, but what I want is a 220 volt kicker adjustment! These are the kind Dr. Morgan gives. I can see why he had such great success, he is so positive about what he finds to adjust and what he can do for me. He has what BJ called the adjustment with that something extra. I had the same thing myself. That is how I know.

What is that something extra? Well, I did not invent this phrase myself. BJ Palmer wrote about this all the time but I don't remember him teaching us what that "extra" really was. I think he wanted us to find out ourselves. I tried to teach my doctors to never just put your hands on the patients and just move their bones. Talk to them about what you find in your leg testing and palpation exam and what has to be done. Let the freshmen in student clinic "adjust and hope," you have to know where the power is shut off (the major subluxations) and what must be done and do it!

I want to get back to my old friends at Lyceum. The reason these chiropractors talk like patients living under the medical tyranny system is because, after a lifetime of encouraging patients to give innate and chiropractic time to get them well, they take on that great importance of looking at treatments for their conditions, the medical side show. That is when they start to let their ticklers die. They have forgotten the principles of chiropractic or they have replaced them with thinking about themselves too much. If you worry about yourself, you will be subject to everyone's opinion of what you should do next and usually these opinions and recommendations are medical. Why? Because they have made a racket out of piece mealing the organs and parts of the body and they get too radical and too aggressive in their practice. That is why there are so many unnecessary surgeries and prescription-addicted people in this nation.

We are their only hope of a drug free life. So senior chiropractors wake up! Get back to the days you thought like a "ten-fingered, two-handed, cure-everything chiropractor!" I still have to encourage my friends to keep thinking like a chiropractor after retirement. They have to keep thinking about what it is that makes chiropractic so great. If they would concentrate on this part of their philosophy, with their hearts or "ticklers," then they would be able to keep the same positive attitude about their bodies as they had when they left school.

What I want them to say is that they are in the best possible shape they can be for their age (65, 75, 85++ and on up) because they keep their subluxations as stable as possible, exercise, eat right and keep the positive mental attitude necessary for mental and spiritual progress. The pioneer spirit and the thought of this progress is what is missing in most old folks. Not me. I need to have an agenda everyday. I need somewhere to hang my hat, some next stop where I can find more fish to fry. These retired doctors should never think their careers are over. I am proof you can keep having a career in chiropractic if you keep giving back to the source.

As I said, "The hole you give through is the hole you receive through." I heard some say at Lyceum that every material thing they have came directly or indirectly from what they learned in chiropractic school. Support that college you went to, or take on a new college, such as Life University in Atlanta, like I did. I got to pull that place up to the standards we all wanted it to have. It was a great opportunity, as I see it!

I think most chiropractors can say when they give back to their alma maters and get involved that they receive a special blessing from God. I really think that the ones who do not give back set themselves up to let their tickler die. I am the kind of guy who wants to see if I can make something happen (remember my axiom? "Them that ask, get. Them that do not ask, do not get.") If it does not happen, it was still a good idea, and I am positive about that. I have miscalculated on investments, but I tried with all my might to make the dominoes fall in order. Sometimes things just don't work out. I don't suck my thumb too long because I look for better fish to fry. If I once get too much into myself, start complaining, start feeling like someone owes me more respect or needs to do something for me then the rug is pulled out and I fall flat on my skinny butt.

So remember, plan something. Plan your work and work your plan, then ask for something else. Nothing begins until you first ask and proceed as if it is going to happen. The last time I heard Dr. Guy Riekeman speak at Life University homecoming, he put a fire into my belly about taking chiropractic on national TV. I remember when BJ used to have a chiropractor give a 30 minute program about the profession every week on his radio station. What ever happened to having us on national TV? Guy wants this to happen. He is the man who can be our spokesperson anywhere in the world.

You see doctors, I don't want you to quit thinking and developing your dreams and goals. Never stop meditating on our great chiropractic philosophy and your personal success philosophy. Don't let age or conditions stop you. I don't want you to ever quit. You must know that no one can or should make you quit or break your spirit. YOU are the only one who can make yourself quit. Suck your thumb for awhile, if you must. Then, get a grip. Get yourself up, into your disciplines and into your mode of progress.

Remember the difference between a giant and a weakling? The giant refused to be a weakling. Read the book of Job. Even when his wife said he should curse God, he said, "We praise God in the good times, why not praise him in the bad times?" You have to refuse to live on the negative side, or to have a poor attitude about life, where you are, how you are doing, what you have to accomplish, how much you are saving. Everyday, write down the "Do Its" for the day and accomplish your goals.

I talked to a retired man who said he was wasting away until his preacher got him delivering Meals on Wheels. When he started going into other people's homes and into their lives, he found more than just the fact that he was far better off in every way than most of these people. He found when he did something for someone, other than himself, each day God gave him more strength, more smiles, more courage, more motivation, and more reason to live. Ask God to not let you waste away in yourself.

Just like this book you are reading, I saw it in my minds

eye long before we started working on it. I may be gone when it is published, but I will smile down from heaven every time you read something and start to pull yourself back up. Pray for this book, that someone else will pick it up at a time when they need encouragement and they will see that Bill Harris overcame many obstacles and so can they.

Faith and persistence: I want it to be the fuel that drives the positive person. All that is needed is to not let your tickler die. Get up, get going, cut your losses if you have to, but turn in another direction and work on that for awhile. Be that positive person, determined to make something good happen in your life. Is it just motivation I am giving you? Maybe, but I like to think it is more. I want you to find power in your life no matter what station you are in at present.

I have known terminally ill people who are positive about the future. I think of the ones who never complained about themselves but rather turned what energy and attention they had left to me and tried to focus on me and encourage me in my life. How can they do this in a terminal state? Well, they developed a positive lifestyle of encouraging people.

My wife was a person like that. She was courageous. When I would leave her bedside, I would walk out in the hall and break down. She would not let me see any state of sadness that her life would be over soon. She was always with me in my life. Jo always wanted me to fulfill my potential more than anyone else. Yes, my dear wife Jo was like that. She battled the tumors until the end and showed me real courage. Every time I came in her room, she wanted to know about my day. She was concerned about my welfare and the children when she was gone. She taught me the meaning of real love for a person. When I was tempted to shake my fist at God and ask why He was taking my wife from me, there was Jo, ready to smile at me and say it would all work out fine in the end and when I got to heaven I would know why she had to go before I did. I am ready for that day.

Listen to the words from this old sage, young women and young men. You are as great as you believe yourself to be. It is time you overcame obstacles, as well as the hurts and depressions that you have allowed to follow you around all your life. These can never build a positive life for you. Don't let the movies and TV shows make you day-dream; those movies where an unrequited love follows a person through life as if to convince the audience this is the way you are supposed to mope and whine around until the day that true love comes back. It is not real life. It is Hollywood. Nothing is real there.

You must leave the past behind. Bad things happen to good people. That can be a great topic of conversation with Jesus when you get to heaven. Good things happen to bad people. Good things happen to good people. Still, here on earth, you must get over unjust times and negative things that are over and done. Just say, right now, they are over and I am going forward in my life now. Let them loose. It is time today that you overcome obstacles in your life. Don't blame parents, bosses, teachers, mentors, lovers, or your genes for the misery you carry around.

If you want to fly with the eagles, you have to climb above your low flying chicken wing attitude. Release everything that keeps you from becoming what you are capable of being. Expand your mind. Read the books out there that will help you do this. Napoleon Hill started this movement with his book *Think and Grow Rich*. Read and study the Holy Bible. Every positive doctrine you will ever need is there for your time and effort. Act as if you are on the greatest journey through life that you can possibly be on today. Act as if you see great potential instead of limitations. Remove the word "can't" from your vocabulary. Also, replace the words "if" with "when." This will get you further up the road. I had to do this everyday for years when the negative thoughts and experiences I went through would invade my day. I am still doing it **right now**!

I read that the average person uses 10 percent of his or her mental powers. To move forward, you have to discipline yourself to pack in more information than 10 percent. This expands your mind and your abilities. Read, read, read. Speak and visit with those who are positive. There are lots of good CDs to listen to when you are in your car. Look for powerful people who can help you create something. Meditate on creating something bigger than yourself. That's what goals are for. When you start on a goal, the most important step is that first small step in your life today. An action step! Even if it's just a better smile or a better golf swing, you have to work at it. It could be a new friend. Write a book, work on an old project. Move ahead mentally and you will move ahead in every other way. Remember this, if you don't move ahead somehow each day mentally and physically, you stand a chance of letting your tickler die. So, keep the tickler going strong. Work on it now! Okay? Okay!

XXII

Action is the Fuel that Fires Your Faith

Show me someone who is always talking about what they are going to do or what they should have done and I will show you a flat lifestyle. The person who takes action is the one moving ahead.

I have found that procrastinators usually fear action steps because of several reasons. First, they think it has to be some great dynamic move forward so they never make the first small step forward. Plus, they set themselves up for failure with inactivity. I can't say it enough for you doctors: it is the small step forward that keeps things growing to bigger and better successes. Next, the doctor may think he has to be a great speaker or a master of spinal screening before he will give a talk or set up a spinal screening. Actually, you just have to try! And then, keep trying and trying and doing and doing.

Aristotle said, "We are what we repeatedly do. Excellence, then, is not an act, but a habit."

It is the action step, regardless of how good you are, that gets you ahead. After you do anything for awhile, you will get better and better. There is a factor besides fear of failure that keeps someone from taking the action steps. It's laziness. Some doctors procrastinate to keep from working. You find me someone who will keep trying, even without much talent, and I will show you someone who is going to succeed. So look into your psyche. Find out what is holding you back. Find a coach and follow their plan for you. Do it! There goes my "Do It" days lecture again.

Why Faith? In this society of ours, you can't mention faith in the same breath as healing or success. Reverend Charles Stanley says faith is the fuel of action. The media does not want you to talk about having religious faith. You see, this is an empirical society and places the most importance on you, the individual. Empiricists want you to think you have to have black and white proof that something will result before you start. They also want you to think that what is proven by science, or what you can see and touch or reason with your finite senses, is all there is. This is bunk.

I know for sure that I did not know how my practice would turn out when I started. I had to walk to the end of the pier and jump in the water. Starting anything new has that element of unknown. I want faith, help from God, with me. Starting my practice was done on faith. I had faith that my education was sufficient and that I had the doctor skills to create a practice. There were no guarantees. I had to try. If I would have looked at my overhead, without any income, I might not have gotten started. But I looked at helping people and I had faith that if I helped one person, they would bring me ten other patients. Plus, I would collect sufficient income to pay my bills and have a good life.

I would hate to have a counting of all the doctors who graduated and never started their practices. It would stagger you. You don't want to know these doctors' failure rate on paying back student loans. I am from the old school. When you borrow money, it is very important to pay it back. I heard some of these doctors tell me they did not know the interest would keep accruing when the loan was deferred. I have also heard some say they thought they did not get their money's worth. However, you signed the loan papers and you must pay off the loan. Being out of debt with no loans will deliver you to freedom. I like that man on the radio today, Dave Ramsey. I strongly advise you to get his books and look at this goal of getting out of debt.

"If you focus on lack, more is taken away.
If you focus on plenty, more is added."

I don't know where I got that saying, but I know as well as I'm sitting here reading this that it is true. Attitude means everything in life. I should have used this sentence to title this book, I use it so much. If you can't get on with having the right faith, with the right actions, with the right intent, you can't move ahead. In business, it is even more critical that you know your product, expenses and markets. Still, there is that area of faith where you have to trust your sales team and the economy to stay at a point where purchases and sales will create a successful company.

In chiropractic practice, you have to see so many patients, perform so many services and collect so much income to be successful. How much is that? Well, that is left open. I know this, when your personal, family and overhead needs are met, you should also be saving 10 to 15 percent and be very thankful. Next, you have to save some of your income to protect yourself in the future. Plus, you have to focus on growth to move ahead of yesterday. If you have leveled off in practice, start saving more and more, because someday you will be burned out in practice.

If you are hiring a coach, wanting more growth, then you are not going into burn out. But, it is just a fact, that you will likely reach a time when you need six months off to re-group and refresh your mind and body. Your chiropractic spirit needs rejuvenating every couple of months. Go to a seminar where service to sick people is the focus. Get with like minds who want to serve. You see, the greatness in chiropractic comes from all the good we have done for people, not by how great we chiropractors are. When your patients esteem you and chiropractic and you are high on their list of important people, then your world changes for the better. I like the little ten words I hear every so often from chiropractors.

"We are changing the world one spine at a time."

I remember a patient who came in with an indignant attitude. She said her brother was coming to me at a reduced rate and she wanted a reduced fee too! We all smiled and said, "Sure thing." That stunned her. She probably was the wealthiest person in the family, but even the wealthy like a deal. At first, this patient thought everything we did in our office was done just for the money. We fooled her! I must have had to give the little brother a break on his fees, I don't remember, but I remember the look changing on big brother's face when he realized my heart spoke to him and that we did all we could do to help people. Our attitude was to give patients way more than they paid for.

Patients have you placed in a position of prominence and/or importance according to how your heart is. This is how you project the reason you are a chiropractor, not so much what you do to help them. You can still charge your normal fees and most everyone will pay, but fees are not what you are about. Fees are the business side that pays the bills. Your fees should be fair and reasonable. What you are really about is changing the world and doing more good than any person you know. Your attitude should be about helping more people than any doctor in your area and giving love and service with a pure, open hearted attitude. You will be getting more money in than most doctors because of this attitude and because you have a large practice.

The only negative that can come in a business sense is when you do not save your income. I will keep saying this to you. Think! Have you ever heard a retired chiropractor say he saved too much money? Remember that doctor who had poor collection systems but thought he could just keep paying the bills every month but not saving for the future? For this doctor that day finally came when there are so many patients who want and need you but you do not have energy to serve them and still not enough money to pay your bills or take time away. So get real smart today. Become a saver. Do like I have suggested before and save 10 percent of everything you take into your office. Put it away and never touch it. When the interest has accumulated, use this to take time away, or to purchase something you want. If you get no financial peace, you will soon lose your practice love and purpose. The money is not the reason you practice, but it is important.

What do you think of being a "healer?" One time I went to a "faith healing" service in a big tent. The man up front was not a famous faith healer, but he was a legend in his area for awhile and his healings had drawn a big crowd that night. I had never been to one of these, so I sat in the back and watched for something fishy (I was like that person who wanted a reduced rate for his adjustment). I wanted to expose the magic side of this service. I moved down front when he started bringing people on stage to heal. What I saw that was real and that I decided to incorporate in my clinic was the anticipation on the faces of the people. They wanted to be healed. How do you create this in your office everyday? This became the Big Question for me to work on.

The first thing I noticed about this preacher was he did not call everyone up on stage and talk about their problems and lay his hands on them. But the ones he did call up had the look of anticipation that something supernatural was going to happen. I saw that same look in some of my new patients. These were often the ones who were referred in by an excited patient who told them I would cure their ailments with the first adjustment. I looked at how to get my patients excited about their results and chiropractic. I always looked in my patients' eyes to see if they were expecting a great event! When I saw that look on their faces, I knew not to talk much, or wrinkle up the anticipation they had for my adjustment.

On the other hand, I did not get frustrated with the many patients who had no faith in me or chiropractic, but who got great results once I cleared them out. Still, I wanted to create a clinic of healing. What I wanted in my office was for the staff and all of us to have that anticipation for what the patient was receiving, knowing that whoever came into our office was going to have a great experience in healing.

This helped me train my staff about innate and how innate healed our patients after I corrected the nerve interference. They could understand that, and then when we had miracles happen, we could celebrate and explain how innate did it. Healing is all a miracle from within. It excited my staff and it excites me today! It helped me to get myself in focus and in tune with my job. It was the catalyst for me to have that adjustment with something special. It was one more dimension for me to focus on for helping sick people.

So much of my work was educating patients to understand how they got well and to understand the greatness in chiropractic. What I found out was the patients did not really care much about innate. They just wanted to get better and get on with their lives. But, even though the patients were not interested in innate and the subluxation, when I focused on this and taught this with fervor, my practice grew and grew. Patients came in to see how much I believed in chiropractic.

I guess patients placed me somewhere in between their medic and that man in the faith healing service. This was a great spot. It was a spot of prominence in their lives. It's the development patients go through in your education process that makes the difference. Some never care about learning or developing in chiropractic. That was okay, I did my best for them too. But, some came to more than one of my new patient classes and read chiropractic books and material and really wanted to learn and develop in chiropractic. So take this thought with you doctor on your healing journey — **do not give up on your quest to get the world adjusted and educated to chiropractic**. The more you work at it, the more your staff or team is creating this anticipation for healing and greatness to happen in your office. As this happens, the more of a chiropractor you become.

XXIII

Put Steam Behind the Dream

I can't tell you too many times how important it is for you to write down your dreams for your practice, your future, your family, your profession, your college, your friends, even your hobbies. This puts steam behind your dreams and ideas and actions. But, here is the key: always write down bigger dreams and goals than you believe you can reach! It costs no more. **You must rise above what you are!**

Remember, we talked about starting small and how to achieve one step toward that goal? That's true, but still you need to make your dreams outside your human understanding. Learn to think outside your capabilities. I know a young man who talks outside his capabilities as well and never achieves what he says he will. Keep these big dreams to yourself and just go to work achieving them.

I told you the story of the doctor who kept raising his fees until almost no one could afford to go to his office? He way over estimated himself! This is not the kind of thinking I want you to do when I say think outside your box. Rather, it is about your capabilities. Think of it as God's talents He gave you. Remember, God gives us raw talents but we have to develop them and devote ourselves to this development.

God thinks about us far above any thinking we can produce. Even past achievements will not carry you. Instead, you have to go above the natural, to the supernatural! It's that saying I like, "If you think you can reach a goal, or you do not think you can reach a goal, you are right." This mean that it's what is above the atlas that keeps you keeping on!

You have capabilities you don't even know you have. I never dreamed I could give a speech until I overcame my fear and started speaking. Oh yes, I had fear when I would speak. This kept me depending on God, but once I got started and made myself speak, I found out, "I was as good as any, and better than most." Now, take these words as a challenge you will accept. I don't know if I enjoy the stress and butterflies until the talk is over and I feel God's pleasure in and through my effort, but I have never given a talk that some good did not come out of it.

Most everyone I coached could not fathom how much talent God has put inside of us and how we hold ourselves back from its development. I spent half my life encouraging doctors to go above themselves. I am encouraging you now. Just believe you can. See yourself as someone in a position you want to be in. Find that person and tell them you want to spend some time with them if they will let you. Tell them you need positive people to encourage you. This is not day-dreaming come true. This is about writing down a goal and working on it and then feeling God's pleasure in what you do. Don't avoid this chance for development. Remember what my Daddy told me, "Do the most difficult jobs first and you will feel the steam behind the dream."

This reminds me of the story of the farmer who got off his tractor and was resting in the cool grass at the side of his plowed field. Looking up in the sky he saw the clouds spelling out the letters "P" and "C." He ran home and told his wife he was supposed to stop farming and "Preach Christ." He started preaching and preaching but he was so bad that finally he could not find anywhere to preach. At last, one day his good friends asked him again about those letters. The friend told him that maybe he should reconsider if the letters might mean, "Plow Corn."

You can go too far to get comfort and change boredom to excitement. You might think you should avoid that hard job.

Like the farmer who should have finished his plowing, you can change directions too quickly. When I started selling practices in Georgia, I talked with doctors who just wanted to change themselves so they thought that meant selling and moving away. I spent most of my time coaching for free to these people because I knew they just needed redirection. Plus, they needed seminars with like- minded doctors to re-charge their chiropractic batteries.

Hidden inside you are great talents that God wants to fulfill through you but you have limited thinking. Let's start today thinking bigger. Anyone can get up each day and go through a routine of things. Learn to give thanks for a good routine. There is great comfort in duplicating your success day after day. You have to motivate yourself to go past routine. Some say boredom comes from not being thankful for your success/routine. I am encouraging you to get up each day and say to yourself, "This can be one of the best days of my life." Tell yourself that this day will be an adventure. Something great will happen. I will give that right adjustment at the right place and at the right time and I will see a miracle! Get up to go on an adventure: ask to stretch above the usual routines of things you do each day; ask to be bigger than you are.

This is how I saw so many miracles in my practice. You do this by writing down your future goals. They represent the big picture of your life now and your life down the road. This is a list you don't have to look at very often. I look at mine once a year at New Year's. What I want you to write down everyday are your "Do It" goals. These are short- term goals that keep your routine in order. These are your things to do today and this week. When someone asks you to give a speech and you have never done it before, say Yes! Learn to scare yourself once in awhile by doing something that will make you stretch and grow.

Everyday start your list off by copying your list from yesterday and putting little notes on your progress with each item. If the item has been done, delete it and bump the next item to the top of the list. This keeps your practice and your life going forward. Remember, sitting still is really going backward. Now, I know everyone has bad days. There are days that seem unfruitful and that is okay. We are not perfect. We have to keep praying to be a better doctor, a better person. We need help, so just ask for it. And don't dwell on those dull days, instead make your list for the next day and go to work!

Today is all you really have. Don't dwell on yesterday too much, just enough reflection to remember your mistakes and to put them in the "Stop This" portion of your brain. Ask yourself not to make that same mistake again. I heard a preacher say the hardest thing for a man to resist is sexual temptation. So if you had a hormone blip about a woman you saw yesterday, put that mistake down on your list to detonate or explode out of your mind. My advice on the sex issue is pretty straight forward. Find a person to marry who loves you warts and all and is excited about changing the world with chiropractic. Then go about the rest of your life being faithful, thoughtful and appreciative of this person.

I have a confession to make to you young doctors today. All my good intentions did not always do it for me. I procrastinate too much on intentions. That is why I write down what I must do, not what I think I want to do. Someone said that along life's way unsuccessful people are filled with good intentions. It is perseverance that counts. Keep on keeping on even when you feel you have come upon too many problems, too many obstacles and defeat has you in its grip.

What I do is give it one more day of my best, then another day, then another. Sometimes, after a few dark days, the light starts to shine, you pull ahead, you begin to make longer strides, you become what you were thinking and working so hard to achieve. It is worth every effort you have. Sometimes, the most successful part of your career comes right after you did not give up.

I have a friend who lost everything he ever had except his loving family. They moved to another state and started over and now he is 100 times the success he was at his last location. Location is not everything in success, but sometimes the freshness of starting over springs you to new heights. I coach my doctors who want to move to a new location very carefully. I read their hearts because I want to see their real intent. I look at their business numbers to see if they are utilizing their current resources. Usually, nine out of ten times, I make them stay where they are planted. I have had so many success stories from my doctors who almost moved away from their future success. If you are thinking these thoughts today, don't move until you have a coach in your corner.

Put this on your long-term goal list. Start a foundation for the future. After I read *Think and Grow Rich* by Napoleon Hill my life started to change. I realized I had positive thoughts but I did not act positively. So I began my quest to become a more positive person. It costs no more and the dividends are great. You must go to the top in positive thinking, but not over the top where you think you are perfect or that everything you think, say and do is 100 percent right. I've seen these people crash and burn. Thinking too much of yourself is fatal because your arrogance will make you fall off the positive thinking mountain. It's steep on the other side.

In his book, Dr. Hill talks about the Rockefeller Foundation. His words spoke to me, suggesting I could start a foundation to help others too. I wrote this down on my goal list that I would someday start a foundation (I even thought of the name FACE, Foundation for the Advancement of Chiropractic Education) and that I would donate more money to chiropractic than any other chiropractor in history. Years later, when I finally started it, I put ten million dollars in the first wave. That is a figure for you to think about. I tell doctors to start their foundations now. This is done with money that is not for you to spend. Open another savings account and start putting money in it each week. Think of a name for your foundation. Start giving the interest to your college research projects when you reach $100,000.00. You will see it does not take long to reach this number. When you retire, you can be like me and spend all your time thinking of how to double your foundation, doubling your profits by giving away more and going from one place to another speaking and accepting the awards and recognition for your gifts. It is fun, fun.

This is something I want you to do today. Don't wait until you reach my age. Start today. All of this you must see yourself doing by using your silent innate mind's eye. Don't tell anyone. Just see yourself getting these jobs done and then go about quality savings and writing your goals and "Do It" list and, day by day, year by year, the miracle of perseverance will take over your dreams. The steam is always in not quitting and in not giving up just because of a limitation. The real steam is your quiet resolve to continue on the road because you know it is right. My prayers and hopes are with you. Begin today.

Get rid of your crabs

I have to talk about crabs again. The crabs in life are like those open tanks of lobsters that are sometimes in seafood restaurants. As soon as one lobster reaches the top of the tank, the one below pulls him down into the morass. I mentioned crabs earlier but not in the context of blowing all the steam out of your dream. They can do it though. Crabs can pull you down into mediocrity when you just get going. They can put negatives into you that keep you from acting. They can draw attention to the "goat feathers" of life that keep you from your mission.

Look for doctors and the type of practices you want to have someday. Visit these practices and get yourself thinking their reality in your own dreams. That is real steam. That is steam that bubbles over into enthusiasm and action, some of the key ingredients that make it happen for you.

I always pitied those doctors whose potential was restricted by a negative spouse. I don't recommend getting rid of your spouse. However, you can't change this person. Only God can. Someone said prayer is the fuel of faith so have faith that they will change for the better. It is something like after an adjustment, the body changes for the better over time. There are non DC husbands who never see the greatness in chiropractic and their doctor- wife's abilities or wives who hold their husband-doctor hostage to their needs first. Some are even jealous of the hold and love chiropractic has over their spouse.

There is usually no way for me to overcome such negatives in a client's life, but when I get them to associate with the type of doctor I want them to be and give them a vision of how their marriage team can be the catalyst behind them, changes do happen. We take on the DNA of our mates. It is just fact. Our voices even start to sound alike. This is very important to think about. Go to marriage seminars if you need to change something about your relationship. Have faith in change for the better. I never give up even when I see such blatant crabs in clients' lives. I look at it as something to really give thanks for when there is a change because marriage is so important.

So stop and look for those crabs in your life. Who is holding you hostage? Who has negative power over you? If you can, get away from friends who do not understand your mission. Stop bringing up your goals around these people. You must know there is a time to hold em' and a time to fold em.'

It is like when I hear people talking about how drug taking makes their body change for the better over time. When I hear these false statements, I start replacing those words in my mind with, "I am praying they will get adjusted, get their subluxations corrected and understand the greatness in God's innate power within us." That makes me positive and I want to be positive.

I talk a lot about steam. I grew up listening to steam train engines chugging by my home. The boiling of a simple thing like water releases this cloud of steam. When channeled into piston chambers it can produce a thousand horsepower to pull a train up a steep mountain. Word power is like this steam to me. Memorize this poem and think of it often, like I do. Remember the poem "Invictus" about being the master of your fate, the captain of your soul. It is only half true because it factors God out of your life and humans are not filled with perfect goodness to be the only "masters of your fate, captains of our soul." We all have dark sides, dark motives. God should be the master of your soul. Your job is to be available with a willing and positive attitude.

> Ships sail east, ships sail west
> By the same four winds that blow
> But it's not the wind or the gales
> It's the set of the sails
> That determines where you go

You have to plan to achieve and work on your distractions and crabs to take discouragement as part of going forward and never give up. Rise above where you are today. I'll be cheering you on!

XXIV

What "Success" Really Means

I tell my doctors they are successful when they deserve it, and not before. Some clients just did not know how to be a doctor and step up and take charge of patients' problems in a positive manner. However, most of the failings I saw in the doctors who signed up with me came from a negative impression they had of themselves. This is what held them back the most (plus their laziness). Many did not receive any love "strokes" and felt victimized by family, patients, spouses and others. They were usually paralyzed or unable to act with authority. They wanted to be loved, but focused on those who treated them poorly, rather than on those who loved them. I tried to love them even when they were convinced they were unlovable. Mostly though, I taught these doctors what success looks like. When they saw they could fit into that success model, they started to change.

There is no other word like success. It is a word or title others give you when you make lots of money or succeed in an area of life. "Loser" might be the opposite. I don't like the word "success" so much. Rather, what I get doctors to focus on is excellence. This is a better word than success. It is a word your hindsight can grow on and a word you can give yourself. It is a word for the hard work and right choices you make each day. You see, excellence is all you have become using the talents God gave you, the education you have obtained, and the choices made from trials and tribulations. Excellence is the result. Excellence is the thing you must succeed in before others should call you a success.

I have seen many servants quietly going about adjusting hundreds of patients without any national or state recognition, yet fulfilling their destiny. These doctors usually are within themselves to the point where they are so proficient and so excellent in their adjusting and patient relationships that they are in demand. This is where I want each client to be. I want patients falling over themselves trying to get under your pisoform. This only happens when you have worked hard to perfect yourself and your skills. Plus, you can see yourself as having reached a new level of commitment. It takes great discipline and the ability to stay focused on your work. Right there you have a great secret in life.

Excellence is not a reward for being very talented. I have seen talented people throw their lives away and squander their opportunities rather than pay the price for excellence. When I see a doctor who wants to achieve a great practice, even though he or she may be low on talent and skill, I know this doctor will make it.

"Wanting to" is more important than the skill level you possess. Is it desire? Is it passion? It is both of these things and more. Still, you have to direct your passion and desire to the right end. I know doctors who love chiropractic and work long and hard on their techniques, but who do not attract patients. When this is the case, I look for laziness or timidity. Sometimes I have found they are hesitant to even introduce themselves as doctor. They have other problems we are not dealing with here.

Excellence doubles its value when it is a team effort. When I see a doctor's family team and office staff/team focused on excellence in chiropractic practice, I see a group who wants to help people. These teams would do any marketing, any talks, any good advertising to get new patients to come to them. When they are trained and committed to giving patients a lot more than they pay for, they get my excellence award. The Eagle Awards were not just handed out at our banquets; they were earned. They were given to doctors who went the extra mile, worked harder than expected and never missed a seminar. These were doctors who wanted to achieve. When they excelled, they were called successful by others, but at Practice Consultants, we saw them become excellent people. These were people I could count on.

To continue to practice in excellence, there must be continued hard work and role modeling. There is no substitute for hard work. Hard work without a plan is wasted energy. I never asked any staff member to work harder than I did myself. Staff will follow your lead if you continue to be fair with everyone. Good things always seem to happen when there is a positive commitment to your plan, followed by hard work.

The biggest commitment is that you and your team really care what is happening in health care in general. Medicine has gotten to be a racket. You and your office must be different than medical clinics. You must be super dedicated to helping people without any hassles or indication that you are working their insurance to make as much off of each patient as possible. That attitude gives off a negative aura or vibes to your patients. You have to have such integrity and intent to help that this takes precedence over every fee, every service and every move you make toward patient care.

You must have a special commitment to educate every patient at your health classes and table talk during each visit. Chiropractic is a health system that is based on something greater than more and more pills and surgery (our natural healing principle that the power that made the body heals the body). It is a system of health! That is why your team must want to get through life without drugs themselves and then be committed to help train patients to substitute the adjustment or natural remedies instead of more and more pills.

The doctor cannot just lead and expect the team and patients to follow. The doctor must be demanding that all office systems reflect excellence. You don't have to be harsh, but you must demand excellence from your staff. If you have a slacker, this person must be let go. I know CAs lose their enthusiasm after awhile. We doctors do, too, but when we step into that office, we have to have a way to gauge our focus and our enthusiasm to educate and help patients. There must be a daily gut check as to why you do what you do.

I am the sort of boss who demands that everyone do their very best. I led by example, never being late, never leaving early, never missing a day, always faithful to chiropractic. I think what I trained everyone to do is to look at the common things you do in the office everyday and learn to do the uncommon. Do more than just say hello when patients walk in. Look at their dress or their smile. Look for what is better about them since you last saw them. Look at their attitude or their character. Look at the chiropractic education you have been giving them in your office. What grade level would you say they are? Are they out of grade school and going higher into understanding of the lexicon, the *Chirospeak*, we talked about earlier?

I can tell you when such a patient leaves your office and goes back to work, she will tell everyone how friendly you are, how helpful, how kind, how much chiropractic is helping her. It all comes from the extra effort, doing more than just the common thing expected from your job.

Teach your staff to set their sights above the ordinary. My CA and Practice Consultants' partner, Dee Warren, was like that. She was an exceptional CA. Later, she helped me with my consulting and when she wanted to do it full time, I knew she would do well because she strived to be more than she was. I helped her learn to speak before a group of doctors and CAs. Soon, she could speak in public much better than I. It was a latent talent she never knew she had and, of course, she was scared like all of us to get up and speak at first. Dee strived for excellence and she was infectious with the clients, motivating them to excellence.

One of my stubborn "hard side" problems was that my team did not know how much I really loved and cared for them. I would forget myself. I would get so involved in the work that my kindness and personal concern for my dedicated team would wane. When that happened, I could always tell because someone in the team would have a "hang dog" expression on her face. Or, I would sense that her bright spirit was dim. When I saw this, I knew something was wrong. I'm sorry for all those people who worked for me and loved me and had to take my hard line demeaning attitude. I never thought of it as abuse, but it really is just that. I did not mean to be so forceful in getting my jobs done. Forgive me, ladies and doctors.

It is an innate thing to be in the back office adjusting all day and to perceive that something is not right at the front desk. It just happens to me. I then have to go and look at the situation. What I find with staff is that they do not want my 99 suggestions, but rather understanding. This is stuff I don't have much of unfortunately. But, I have tried to be gentle and more understanding. Still, I fail.

I guess I gave what "soft" stuff I had to patients, because when I got home, my wife would tell me I talked more gently to patients than I did to her and the kids. That was true for me, but you do not have to be this way. So, develop a work ethic for your team that creates excellence and discipline and motivates them at the office and throughout their lives. They will thank you later. Later, much later, maybe someone will call you "successful." But here's a word of caution: don't read your own press clippings!

XXV

The Big Picture

I want every doctor to see the big picture of his or her life. I talked about making "treasure maps." Do you remember these? Each doctor who entered my consulting program was asked to clip out pictures of places and things he or she wanted in life and stick them on a poster board, making a map of the desired future in pictures.

Jesus used word pictures better than anyone in history. I can see Him looking at the fig tree that did not bear fruit as He related this to the self-centeredness of the Pharisees who thought they were producing godliness. We have to look at our spiritual maturity, our families, our practices, and the future of our profession as something we are taking into consideration every time we give an adjustment. Every time we make a decision that will impact our families and profession, it must have a futuristic intent. It must not be for us alone! It must be for others. That is the big picture you must look at each day of your life.

I remember talking to an officer of a liability insurance company who told me 90 percent of malpractice claims are a result of a financial problem with patients. In most cases, he said, all the doctor would have had to do is call the patient and work out the money grievance. But no, the staff and doctor had to be "right," and thus the law suits would follow. You have to look toward the future of your practice and life. I know there are necessary trial cases where people are injured in various ways, but I have not seen much good come from suing people. Only the lawyers win in lawsuits.

Most of these accounts payable cases had to go through court trials or depositions and, later, settlements that emotionally and financially stalled lives and practices. Make sure your malpractice insurance is up to date, but try to settle disputes yourself. Stay out of court if you can and deal with the present as you want it to impact the future of your practice.

The same goes for your personal life and the future of our profession. Retired people should get out of the big homes where they raised their families to lower their space, stress, and responsibilities and simplify life as they age. It should be the same with your practice. I see doctors who had big, multi-doctor clinics who sold these high-stress locations to start over and scale down to just one doctor and one CA working limited hours. Now that is smart. I can't tell you the number of practices I've looked at where the doctor should have sold out years before. Your last decade in practice should be low stress and fun, even if you are eighty years young!

One of the best things a doctor can do besides having weekly staff meetings with the office team is to make an Office Policy book. Start by writing your opinion of how your team will handle emergency visits, cash patients, PI patients, WC patients, MM insurance cases, inebriated patients, hostile patients, money grievances, vacations, time on the phone for personal calls, maternity leave, raises, job descriptions, accidents in the parking lot and office, cross training, and every other aspect of dealing with employees and patients. The key to management from a doctor's standpoint is to be consistent, knowing every policy and job description and not playing favorites, bending the policies, or making unilateral decisions. As the boss, you have to be consistent in all you do. You must come on time, be caught up on your paper work, be present for staff meetings and lead the charge. You must always give training sessions and philosophy talks to your staff.

Next, evaluate your office and service and keep moving the standard higher and higher each year. That is how you grow and become more than you think you can become.

Step up above the average doctor. Average doctors with average practices live to put in their time, make a nice living and that's it. You can't do this and grow. Just putting in your practice hours like it says on the sign out front won't make it happen. If you are a new doctor, use your cell phone. Pick a "marketing day" and tell your CA to call you if a patient comes in. Then go out and talk to people about what chiropractic can do for them and give out your office packet. Cluster book your appointments and put in your office time adjusting, not playing on the internet.

You have to put first things first. Your primary priority for increased practice growth is new patients; this one factor determines growth. Of course, you have to look at patient compliance, education, retention, patient visit average, collection percentage, and dollar amount collected per visit to see if your office systems are up to peak performance, but mostly you have to take new patients into your practice on a regular basis.

You must ask your team what is important to them in their work. You will see that it is usually the same thing that is important to you. If it is not, then you have just been putting in your time and going along, hoping against hope that everything will turn out okay in the end. That is what I call pantheism or the belief that everything will pan out in the end! It is not the thing that will work for practice excellence.

When you look at your monthly practice stats you are looking at your self assessment. If they are down, or showing downward trends, you are the reason, doctor. It is not that some team members have slipped down, but that you have not encouraged them to excel. Even if your clinical practice is excelling, you keep checking on your practice systems to know if you are sticking to your plan and purpose. Your stats are the measurable results of sticking to your purpose and disciplines.

Today, be honest about where you are in practice and where you would like to be. If you are at a standstill, maybe you need a coach. If you know you are not doing what you should be doing, get to work and coach yourself onward and upward! You doctors who own your own business have no excuses. Don't blame the economy, the factory shutting down and whatever else others blame for the sluggishness in their lives. There is never a shortage of subluxations or patients who need adjusting — never! There are only barriers to new patients coming in for care.

I have proven this to be true in many ways and in many times. When my entire city was paralyzed by negative news, my practice grew because I did not listen to the news and I focused on the stress I felt in my patients who accepted the negatives, or were spreading them. If they needed two adjustments in a day, I only charged for one. People in stress need adjustments more at that point than any other time. It was the same during the holidays. My practice boomed at holidays because of the stress and the need I felt when I examined my patients during these periods. I scheduled more visits to get them through the holidays. Your stats tell you the trends of your office. If you want to grow, tell the team what you want the stats to look like and share solutions with them. Then work your plan. Set small steps up the ladder for achievement and provide bonuses so they can share in the growth.

I heard of a doctor who kept a journal each day. He would write down the part in practice he felt edified him and things that perplexed him about that day. He would mentally thumb through each system in the office and then make plans in his journal. It worked for him. I couldn't do this much myself. Maybe if you can't write down your "Do It" list each day, consider keeping a short-term journal. One thing a journal will do is keep you organized. If you feel unorganized then make this a "Do It"! You have to have a certain time to write in the journal every day or you won't get it done. That alone will help you organize your office.

One thing I recommend you do each day is end on a positive note. I know animal trainers who teach animals through continual repetition who say they have to end the training sessions on a smooth, effortless, positive experience. If not, the animal may sour to training and start digressing. If you end by scolding the animal, then at the next contact, they start out feeling scolded. The same is true with your staff. If they are having a tough day, spend a few moments with them before they leave and see that they leave on a positive note. I am convinced people do not get enough positive strokes. Everyone wants to feel significant and appreciated. So take a minute to do this. If nothing else, it lets that person know you thought enough to attend to the situation, even if you can't change things.

The same is true with you. You have to leave your office like you show up in the morning, with a positive frame of mind. You know this happens when you have that pleasant, tired feeling in your gut (and feet). End with a positive mind set, or a vision of how you wanted the day to go in your mind (visualize all those patients coming in). You want to feel a relaxed peace that comes with a job well done. It is a great benefit from chiropractic that you can get this peace from helping others. It is a gift from God to you doctors, so don't take it lightly.

I remember coaching a doctor who was hiring a front desk person. Of course, I recommend cross training but this was not the need he had in his office. I told him in the interviews to ask candidates who balanced the check book at home. If they admitted they were poor at this, chances are high they would goof up your day sheet and your finances. It is the same with training yourself to do jobs you have not been good at before. You have to change how you do them. To change yourself, you have to want to do better. If you are poorly organized, it will be difficult to organize your staff, or to get an agenda for your meetings with your office team. But if you make yourself do this for a long, consistent time, you will be better organized in other areas of your life that were lacking before. That is one of the keys to moving ahead. Don't hold yourself back because you have accepted a lack in your life.

Now, if you can't carry a tune in a bucket, don't join the choir. But in office management, you have to make yourself be the boss. There is no other way. Do this by getting good staff members to continually give you reports on what is going on in the office. If you work hard at this, not only will the office efficiency increase, but the team members will be more organized, more punctual, and more goal oriented than they have ever been before. I have had more than one office staff member tell me that, by working in our office, it helped her or him run the family more efficiently. Teach your team to plan, set goals, and work together in events like Patient Appreciation Days. Let them solve problems, set schedules and generally feel they are a part of a highly successful and productive practice. Remember, this is the way you must feel, so they have to feel like you do. Go to it. Don't delay or show neglect. This would exhibit a lack of maturity. You must be the leader.

XXVI

My Texas Romance

I just got back from the Texas Chiropractic College president's retirement banquet. I gave $480,000 to this college and do not regret a nickel. I do not regret it mainly because they did not just take my money and go on as usual. They did what I said to do to make this money produce more income and benefits for the students and the college. It worked and the college is moving ahead today better than ever.

At this banquet, they were celebrating the retiring president Shelby Elliott. He was the one who got me to donate and he is the one who wanted me to speak. Dr. Shelby had a long history of service with the ACA and I had watched his presidency and seen his productivity.

Many years earlier, I was speaking at Life Chiropractic College West and Shelby was there. He had just accepted the position as president of Texas College. I knew this, but did not know the college was in trouble financially. Donations were not coming in and the student enrollment was at an all-time low. Shelby kept following me around. When he got the chance to speak to me, he told me he wanted me to donate to the college. I asked him why. It was at this time that his face took on the look of a beagle dog I used to have. It was such a sad face that I felt instant compassion in my heart for the man. Later, we sat down and talked. He admitted to not having a lot of experience with college work. He just loved his alma mater and felt that if Texas went under, not only were the alumni's diplomas devalued, but that a great loss would accrue to the profession and to him personally.

This was the start of my romance with the college. He needed me to donate, but I wanted to put more than supports on his college. I mapped out a little plan for him that night and told him, if he made it happen, I would give him the money for the college to survive for a few more months. He said he would do what I said to the letter and he did! Here is what I outlined for him:

• Have all the staff and faculty read *Think and Grow Rich* by Napoleon Hill and write down how these success principles can help the college move forward. Next, he was to meet with every department head to look at their systems and see where the negative attitudes were and what was holding the college back internally. Then, he was to present plans for every department to move ahead. Progress was the only thing he was going to understand and tolerate. Every department was to increase productivity and all department heads must focus on increasing enrollment and enhancing the college's image in students' minds.

• A ten year plan was to be on my desk in a week and then I would cut the first check.

• He was to hire a fund raiser and developer who had faith in this college and base his salary on production; we were talking about survival and showing increase.

• He was to put a new coat of paint on the walls (get the students involved) and buy some new furniture to show the students he was concerned about the college and the pride he showed would transfer to the students. He could not lose his pride in his school and must figure out how to pass it on.

• He was to control the budget himself and be responsible for needless spending. Every department would cut expenses and tighten their belt until solvency.

• He was to have a new motto for the staff and faculty, "Faith is the muscle that grows your belief."

• He was to get rid of doomsayers and look for those with the faith to pull out of this slump.

• He was to think like Samson, that God gave him his strength and power. He would call several alumni every day and be excited about all this college means to them and get something donated to the school from each one.

He went home and went to work!!

Dr. Elliott built four new buildings on the campus during his tenure and made his college a fine learning institution. He is to be congratulated and praised for his work. My money helped get him over the hump. He says it saved the college. I don't know about that for sure, but their change in attitude and work ethic did a lot more in the long run than my money.

I told the crowd at that dinner that this was the worst food I had ever eaten but the most expensive dinner I ever paid for! They laughed, but really I am glad to have had a small part in this endeavor.

Pulling the college out of disaster was like helping doctors come up out of the ashes of failure. It is never easy. It takes a new attitude and fortitude to keep on keeping on, as BJ used to say. Plus, you have to have a plan and work your plan untiringly. If you are reading this today and feel your practice and your professional life slipping away, take notice. Chiropractic has not failed you. But, you must put life supports on a slipping practice.

One time, I talked with a new grad who was a physical therapist before becoming a chiropractor. He said he was now practicing PT but adding adjustments and he wasn't sure about his technique. Somewhere along the way his compassion for chiropractic got hung up. He must look at why he became a DC. He must know and feel that he gained more than just one more therapy. What's missing here? Why was his practice and desire to help people flat? I think it was because he did not have a defined purpose for his work. He did not feel a mission, or a movement to talk to patients about how innate changes them from the inside after the adjustment.

You have to want to change people and the world, to make things different than medicine. He lost the inspiration he started with. I've seen this happen time and time again. If I could tell young doctors anything today and get it to stick, it is to believe what we know about innate healing in chiropractic to be true. You must **believe** in the self healing mechanism and practice with a purpose that is bigger and more important than yourself. You don't have to understand everything about innate's work in our physiology. We use a remote to change TV channels and I don't understand at all how it works. I don't understand how the engine of my car works, and I don't want to, but I have faith that it does work. Look at innate self healing the way we look at the law of gravity. We expect the law to work and we believe in it to work. Put this vision of health and where it comes from into each patient and put it in them with passion and a firm resolve. Then, you will have created a cadre of patients who want what you have. You have so much to give to patients, more than can always be understood intellectually.

I remember a patient who came out to the front desk after the adjustment and told the CA I had broken her back. She said she had a broken back one time and she knew it was broken again and that I did it. It did not matter that she was a mentally challenged person. She still upset my staff and those in the waiting room. She was going on and on so they came and got me. I called up the hall to her and motioned for her to step inside a room with me. She calmed down and I kept talking to her. Here was my script, "You do not have a broken back. I have gone to school and studied many years to learn how to adjust and help spinal problems like yours and you do not have a broken back. You will be better after my adjustment. I will call you tonight and check on you; count on this. I want you to promise not to go around telling people I broke your back. Your x-ray revealed several spinal bones that are fixed together, but I can help them too. Now, you just do what I say and you will find out in time that your back will be much better than it ever has been in years and years. Plus, I plan a rehab program that will help your back get stronger so your years ahead will be much better because you take adjustments."

The woman calmed down and left. I called her that night and gave her some more encouragement and some home care advice. She returned the next day with a better attitude and became one of the best patients I ever had. She referred many patients and the first thing she told her referrals was that I studied long and hard to learn how to help backs like hers and I was the best. This is the type of firmness you need to have in your gut regarding what you are doing. You are here to do more than just help patients get out of pain. You are to watch them change over time, through regular adjustments, to come to a better place anatomically and physically than they ever could have come to without adjustments.

Believe in your adjustments and in innate to heal and change your patients for the better over time (the big idea). You have to step out in faith if clinical results are all you have to back you up at this time. I'm counting on your children to have the research to back them up. Until that time, work with all the positive intent you can muster to build value as you encourage patients. Celebrate what you do each day and how it changes the world, making it a little bit better day after day. It may take a few lifetimes to understand all the good chiropractors have done all these years.

XXVII

Learn the Innate Philosophy

The chiropractic innate philosophy, "There is an innate intelligence in all living things that maintains it in existence," became very important to me. I taught my patients the key to health as staying as subluxation free as possible each day so innate can change me for the better over time. However, there are many successful doctors I have coached who were not taught this innate philosophy and have done just as well as anyone else in practice. It's possible to be a good clinician and help many people yet not think in only one, specific way (i.e. innate philosophy or bust!).

That separatist attitude split the profession for decades. I say, celebrate the fact that you can be either one or both as a clinician. If your mind is only on getting the patient to feel good again (over their acute pain) then you have to watch that your patients are just short-term, pain–fix and then they will be gone. If you like this type practice, you have to have a ton of new patients but this type of practice fits some doctors' attitudes and they are very successful.

If you are into the innate philosophy, you will feel a desperate need to tell all patients that everyone needs to be as subluxation free as possible for the rest of their lives. These patients are your maintenance or lifetime patients.

Both types of practices are good, and my coaching was to have my doctors do whichever type fit them the best. I urged them to offer the best, but accept what the patient is able to pay for. I never kept any part of chiropractic from either one of these patient groups. I took them all to the most benefit from being under my care whether they were short-term or lifetime patients. Why? Because you never know which patient will stay for life, so I put all my seeds in the ground and watched them sprout and grow.

I always start out with new patients as if they were short-term, quick-fix, acute care patients only. Then, after the first or second adjustment and they were really testifying for me, I would do the report of findings. New patients can't have much respect for you and chiropractic until they get results. I found, after a couple visits, they listened better when they trusted me and knew I could really help them get over their conditions.

If you concentrate only on treating pain, inflammation and joint immobilization problems, etc., with therapies and treatments of a natural sort, you don't have to be concerned with the innate philosophy. That's okay with me too. I just like talking about this innate vital force, and how Vitalism is a part of chiropractic from the beginning and how you can put more faith in innate than in synthetic, dangerous drugs. It's okay if you don't want to change the world. You can be the best doctor out there and that is what draws patients and success to you.

I guess I inherited the missionary flavor in school so I had to "convert" my patients. This is the way I live my life and that is what I tried to teach every patient and client. I think my old school ways are still good. DD and BJ Palmer used innate to identify the "doctor inside" that got results following their adjustments. They talked about moving bones in a cadaver, but nothing would happen. The life force was gone.

I liked to teach that innate is a power source you can depend on for internal health, but that you must couple this with good nutrition, exercise and a positive mental attitude to keep your body changing for the better over time (always teach that chiropractic is about mind, body, spirit). There is something mystical in this slant, but miracles happen when you adjust a vertebra in a patient. To me, as a young man coming to chiropractic school as a career, this was like stepping into a philosophy discussion with two different sides. No one was sure what the doctrine really meant for either one. In my school, innate was important. In others, innate was not important and not even taught. Even in my philosophy classes, many did not like it. To others in my class, the philosophy was what they lived for.

For some in the profession who liked to lean toward religious fervor, philosophy about innate became a mantra to separate themselves as having secret knowledge that other chiropractors lacked, or were not strong enough to verbalize and practice. This thinking and separation is what has caused the schisms in our profession. One truth is for sure: you don't have to live in the innate philosophy of chiropractic to help your patients get well. To me, the innate philosophy gave me more power to add to my adjustment. It was this innate power trapped, if you will, in the subluxaton. When I exclaimed that, "I turned the power on!" I found that the more belief I had in the adjustment and the body's self healing mechanisms, the greater my patients followed me and referred others to me.

I think when you have more faith in innate than in drugs and medical doctors, you start to live at that healing point where patients can follow you. I never put this philosophy into a new patient at first. When new patients come in your office, you have to stick with their pain and symptoms on the first visit so they can see you want what they want (to get better). Even though the patient hears your words about the subluxation and what the adjustment will do for them, still it is the music from your heart that they are really listening to. That provides an intuitive prompt that you know what you are talking about that, coupled with relief provided from the first adjustment, gets you well on the way to creating a chiropractic patient. If you are hesitant and unsure of results, and don't know in your heart that innate can cure them, this too comes into their psyche like a crashing cymbal. **Build confidence first!** Then, see if they will listen to what chiropractic is all about. I'll say it again! Get the patient in your confidence, then start taking the patient into the area of healing, more faith in innate, subluxations and changes within the body only innate can make.

I wanted to put medicine in that place where we fear dangerous synthetic chemicals and have more respect for innate and adjustments. Yes, I refer to MDs in emergencies and trauma. But this is not tied to where health originates. Patients with chiropractic knowledge and faith stay for life or, even if they quit care, they know what chiropractic can do and what it is all about. Make sure of this point! Yes, they are affected by the world and will go back to the medics. Don't let that make you negative. Instead, make this fact all the more important in your patient education systems.

With new patients in the beginning, I start talking body mechanics, neurophysiology (electrical problems), weight bearing surfaces, and negative spinal orthopedic changes I want to correct. On subsequent visits, the lecture for new patients delves into innate, subluxation, adjustment, leg testing, muscle testing, thermography, EMG testing, scans, etc. Words can mark a switch from medical/pharma brain washing. My goal was to create a vacuum that can only be filled by an interested and grateful patient. This is one who has more respect for chiropractic than for me, or all that I have done for them. I am always waiting for this point in their experience. Some patients become respectful to chiropractic in a powerful way. Like me, they become thankful for chiropractic. I always want to ask those who understand, "What has innate done for you today?" To me, that is a powerful point of discussion and a lofty goal to shoot for in patient care.

I am asked a lot about what I think of BJ's books wherein he made innate into a sort of deity. The "fellow within" sort of looks like innate is BJ's spirit guide telling him what to do. This is not what DD Palmer wrote or talked about. BJ made this part of the innate doctrine. But even BJ made sure Stevenson's textbook on chiropractic philosophy (1927) did not depict innate as a deity, but rather as an intelligence that is in control of all physiology.

It was in the 1930s that BJ started the "fellow within" doctrine. In Stevenson's textbook, God was called Universal

Intelligence and referred to the same way in class. Innate is a part of Universal. Stevenson's book was the standard text at Palmer for the BJ years. It was Stevenson who wrote that the PhC thesis could not compare innate to a god or religion.

I don't know what got into BJ to write and lecture about innate as a person. Why did he make all this personal spirit guide stuff up? It was like he wanted to separate himself from all the other chiropractors in the world because only BJ had this secret knowledge about innate. The time frame was after he went around the world and studied the eastern philosophies. So maybe it was just his ego that had to show that he had secret knowledge about chiropractic and innate that others did not have. If his intent was to separate himself from everyone else in the profession, this innate separateness attitude surely did this.

I think it was a mistake for BJ to be so insistent that innate philosophy be taught in every school the same way he taught it. Of course, these other schools went the opposite way from BJ. It will be interesting to watch history and see where it takes us on this subject. However, my respect and love for BJ has never waned. BJ was my teacher and mentor. To me he is still the greatest chiropractor who ever lived. There was no person then or now who impacted the profession more than BJ did. He was a tireless worker. He never stopped trying to get the subluxation and adjustment down to the science of his day.

I feel I am carrying on BJ's work when I donate to our research. I believe chiropractic would not be around today if it were not for BJ and his relentless work to defend and educate chiropractors. If you are weak on your philosophy or you went to a college where they taught no philosophy, then chances are you left your college thinking that manipulation was just another natural adjunct to use in treating pain and symptoms. This type of thinking to me takes all the power and dedication to the healing miracle out of chiropractic. However, it does not mean you can't be a great success.

I think it's ironic that, while some chiropractic schools disdain innate, medicine is looking into prayer, meditation, music, magnets, faith healing, manipulation, massage, acupuncture, and everything else imaginable that affects healing within the patient other than medicine. Why? Because it is popular and people are seeking out alternative, non-medical doctors so medicine wants to cash in.

I sure do not understand why some chiropractic colleges still want to pound on the point that they teach no philosophy, only "research based" chiropractic, and disdain our historical innate philosophy. The animosity that BJ caused could be one answer. I say, let's get together and go along with chiropractic research. Everyday our research proves that adjustments do more than help just backaches and headaches. All natural healing aids are good, as long as they are organic and help innate change the patient for the better. We are not here to just treat pain until it is better. We are here to celebrate the miracle of healing, and prove we know what we are talking about. It's just a matter of time, I think.

Our innate philosophy gives more understanding into the miracle of healing than any philosophy out there in the health sciences today. Why not learn it and dedicate your professional life and mission to making a better world without drugs? Why wouldn't you want to change the world? Why wouldn't you want people to embrace the understanding of innate? Why wouldn't you want people to depend on innate instead of just another pill? We are the only ones teaching how to keep your bloodstream pure. That alone must keep us separate from medicine. What about internal physical fitness, instead of internal pollution? That is the music you need to be singing beneath your words and procedures. Sell out to this philosophy of changing patients for the better over time! Sing this innate music of dedication in your heart and look for this singleness of purpose to bring you more power and hope for chiropractic. Remember, patients pick up on this in your office. It is why I was so successful and why patients stayed with me for life.

So, if you have not before, decide today to learn the innate philosophy. If you do, you will learn something bigger than yourself, bigger than your doctoring ability and bigger than bone moving that takes place after your adjustment. It will be our truth to put all your faith into for healing. Innate can be relied on, worked with and given credit for healing. Patients can thank you for adjusting them and making them feel better, but they must know that, "The power that made the body is what heals the body."

Chiropractic must be more than just another treatment for symptoms. We have a healing system with innate at the helm. Let's exploit this to the world. Innate is the life force breathed into us at birth. Remember, this is natural law. Like gravity, innate is working now, inside of you, whether you like it or not. Whether you think you can use it or not, it is still working. That is why everyone can get results adjusting at the right place, at the right time. So, whether you teach innate healing to your patients, or even care about it yourself, innate is still at work, getting the results you desire. You have to decide to take the credit for the healing or give it to innate.

Let's go deeper in this innate philosophy. I think you have to watch talking about innate so you don't make chiropractic into some type of religion. There are doctors who teach innate and appear to be off the deep end. I cannot defend these people who take the profession to the edge of cultism. Tom Morgan, who is helping me write this book, also wrote a book where he discussed taking innate one step too far. I think doctors who do this do an injustice to the profession, as well as to their patients. I would go one step further and say we need to get spiritualism doctrines or teachings out of the profession.

I have heard chiropractors say the adjustment connects the spiritual with the physical. This concept is not taught at any chiropractic college. It is a made up philosophy coming from seminar speakers, not from our colleges. The profession as a whole does not embrace this connection. I can see where you could make up such a doctrine because of that spirit part within the human body, but this doctrine does not belong in the chiropractic profession. Innate cannot be seen. Rather, it is like electricity, an intelligent energy. Chiropractic, as a profession and not a church, must teach and understand it in the context of physiology. Innate is making your heart beat at this moment. This energy working through the nervous system can be embraced and taught without religious connotation. We must teach and understand that electric current can toast my bread in the toaster, but this energy is not speaking to my conscience mind, telling me what to do. I believe we can depend on and understand the action or function (physiology) of innate. Let us live in this understanding and not make our innate philosophy some "fellow within."

When I sat in philosophy class at Palmer, the excitement we experienced was the music we carried out to our practices. Innate was the exciting understanding that separated us from non-natural healers. We would sit in the cafeteria and discuss this innate concept for hours. It still is exciting to me. There was no discussion on having faith at the college, but it was this faith in innate to change our patients for the better after the adjustment that was our rallying point. It was the reason we adjusted and the reason to watch innate mechanisms heal the patient. It made the subluxation have dynamic meaning. We were not just mobilizing joints like the medics said we were doing. Instead, we were adjusting to normalize the entire neurobiomechmechal systems so innate could begin its trek back to homeostasis. It made us want to be a different type of doctor. It made us proud that only chiropractors are able to locate and correct subluxations with such a high level of expediency. It made us want to understand all the sick people getting well as a result of correct adjustments and innate healing. It made us excited about creating research aimed at understanding nerve dysfunction caused by the subluxation and thus limiting innate's capabilities at the cellular level. The field is wide open to this research today. In fact, research is the hope of the profession, and maybe our entire destiny!

Before we leave the innate philosophy, let's speak to this doctrine of innate speaking to you inside. As we mentioned, the peripheral meaning of innate speaking to you inside was just an offshoot of BJ Palmer's "fellow within" doctrine. BJ's concepts created much excitement, but were very problematic. BJ wanted to create an uproar in the profession much like the one he created when he wrote and lectured that chiropracTIC is greater than medicine, greater than law and greater than religion. I don't think BJ had all the answers to everything. Rather, I think his motive for such flamboyancy is couched in the political idea that his followers had special knowledge which the rest of the profession did not have.

Some of the made up doctrines of BJ are still talked about today. It was not healthy when BJ made them up and it is not healthy for our profession to be teaching them today. Why would chiropractic ever want to join or circumvent religion? What would there be to gain if our profession leaned more toward the spiritual rather than on the life sciences, techniques and principles already established in the profession today? Innate is an intelligence, not a dogma. We don't want to be saying that innate was the same as Jesus or Mohammed or connected to some religion's teachings. This was only an idea of BJ's. It was not grounded in physiology and natural laws, as innate must be grounded.

My fellow church going friends in school were turned off by substituting innate for a person, prophet or god. My goal was to understand innate and celebrate innate as the intelligence that controls physiology. Innate added on to the religion I believed in and practiced. I had more faith in my adjustment than my friends because of my faith. But it did not make chiropractic my religion. We must keep innate out of religion and put it where I think it belongs; at the top and center of our healing philosophy. To do otherwise, would lump a licensed healing profession in with New Age religion.

This talking spirit guide idea for innate sounds like New Age religious philosophy and these types of speakers in our profession are not grounded in chiropractic principles or the Koran or the Torah or the Christian Bible. These people who would distort our innate philosophy show disrespect to religions, as well as to chiropractic. We must never get into the cult issue of making chiropractic a religion. Instead, we must celebrate our innate philosophy and agree that innate is not just nature or some blind energy within each of us, but an all powerful intelligence which knows the difference between a red blood cell and a white blood cell.

Innate cannot function normally with a subluxation present. The control mechanisms of innate intelligence become distorted, decreased, or impeded when a subluxation is present. The adjustment corrects a cause of dysfunction by normalizing the neurobiomechanical systems. Of course, we have new nomenclature on innate today, and we know a lot more about the role innate plays in adaptation to the environment, immune competency and to psychic problems. But we are still in agreement with our founders that subluxations come from physical trauma, psychological imbalances, and toxic changes from ingested chemicals. Every chiropractor who has practiced very long knows that innate can take the right adjustment at the right place at the right time and produce a modern day miracle! Also, we know that having a regular adjustment schedule over the long term is the most beneficial service we have to offer, as well as the one that is the least utilized by patients.

So doctors, learn the innate philosophy of healing. This is an important part of our past and future; there is power in this philosophy. It can spark your practice. Start giving your innate talk to patients at the New Patient class or as they come in for care. Get them to see your mission and the movement you are creating in your community.

I see the words "practice members" in print from the coaches today. It is a good term as these members take part in something bigger than the doctor and bigger than themselves; they are part of a health movement. This is a powerful understanding and system away from pills and surgery. This is a movement based on the truth about health and where it originates. It is about innate and the vitalistic, self recuperative power of the body.

Chiropractic is a celebration of this natural law of life. I encourage you to teach how to live each day taking into account daily disciplines that help innate change the organism to a better point than yesterday. Yes, learn about innate, learn to teach innate and you will be given a greater appreciation of how you were made and how this healing principle was given to the world through our science. We are here for our practice members, not ourselves, to show them healing and how we practice a system that is natural and designed to help our bodies every second of our lives.

Additional copies may be purchased for **$20.00** each by contacting:

Life University
Development Office
1269 Barclay Circle
Marietta, Georgia 30060
(800) 543-3436 / (770) 426-2975

We accept checks, VISA, MasterCard and American Express

NAME_____

ADDRESS_____

CITY _____ STATE_____ZIP_____

PHONE_____

EMAIL _____

CARD NUMBER _____

EXPIRATION_____ SECURITY NUMBER_____

The Red Hat Scholarship has been endowed at Life University to help chiropractic students who need financial support to complete their degree program. Every contribution is matched by the Harris Family Foundation. Please give to the Red Hat Scholarship and support a future chiropractor that needs your support.

NAME_____
ADDRESS_____
CITY _____ STATE_____ZIP_____
PHONE_____
EMAIL_____
CARD NUMBER_____
EXPIRATION_____ SECURITY NUMBER_____
DONATION AMOUNT _____
PAYMENT: OneTime_____ Monthly_____ Annual_____

CPSIA information can be obtained at www.ICGtesting.com
Printed in the USA
243523LV00001B/7/P